A SPORTING WANDERER

A Sporting Wanderer

GORDON ALLAN

THE Alpha PRESS

Published by

The Alpha Press
18 Chichester Place
Brighton BN2 1FF

First published 1995

ISBN 1 898595 12 7

Copy-edited and typeset by Grahame & Grahame Editorial, Brighton
Printed and bound in Great Britain
by Antony Rowe Ltd, Chippenham, Wiltshire

Contents

Acknowledgements

I wish to thank Lucy Barker and the National Exhibition of Children's Art for permission to reproduce the poem "Bowling Green".

My thanks also to *The Times* newspaper for permission to reproduce excerpts from material previously published.

The permission of Sport & General, and John Beasley, to reproduce the text photographs is acknowledged.

Cover design is by Ian Wileman.

It is no wonder, therefore, that a subject about which most of us have some knowledge, and which arouses such intense interest in so many people without creating any permanently bitter feeling, is grasped as a bridge between one man and another. Arguments about politics or religion make one feel the differences between one's self and one's neighbour: sport makes one able to realise one's kinship.

J. P. W. Mallalieu, *Very Ordinary Sportsman*
(Routledge & Kegan Paul, 1957)

I have come to feel a deep, unspoken pity for people who have no attachment to a single sport.

Alistair Cooke, *Fun and Games with Alistair Cooke*
(Pavilion Books, 1994)

1

Introduction

In 1965 I joined *The Times* as a sports sub-editor, reporting on rugby on Saturdays. I resigned after eight years but continued to work for the paper as a freelance. During the 1980s I began writing regularly on bowls and for a while turned out a weekly column on various topics loosely related to sport. It is from those years that the bulk of the material in this book is drawn.

Writing a newspaper column is enlightening. I used to think that the first and most valuable lesson a columnist learns is that nothing he or she writes has the slightest effect on anybody or anything. But this is not so. If the reader only yawns and turns the page, it is still an effect of a sort.

Three readers of a piece I wrote about a vacuum cleaner tycoon (included in this book) did not yawn and turn the page, but digested every word, and took the trouble to ask me about the man, who wanted to sponsor a sport but could not find one suitable because he insisted that it must have a clear affinity with vacuum cleaning. Two of the readers wrote to me with suggestions, including marathon running – "a long, dusty business". One said she was a member of the Great Britain women's powerlifting team. The third buttonholed me at a press conference. All three evidently believed that the vacuum cleaner tycoon was real. I had to inform them, with profound regret, that he was not. He was invented for the purposes of the article. While the article lasted, he lived and laughed and loved. With its final full stop he died. I was sorry to see him go. I felt we had much in common, and I was proud of him. A journalist has few chances to be creative, but for five minutes or so I created a vacuum cleaner tycoon, and made him live for three readers at least. No Pooter or Forsyte he, and I never claimed immortality for him. He was just an ordinary, hard-working, law-abiding, God-fearing vacuum cleaner tycoon, faithful to his wife, devoted to his children, and a twelve-handicap golfer.

There is a lesson in that tale. Sport divides – think of soccer hooligans; and sport unites, which is a far more widespread result. If my vacuum cleaner tycoon had been real, he would have met these readers, and they would have enjoyed each other's company because they had in common one of the most universal of subjects.

Playing sport, talking about it, arguing about it, reminiscing about it, even reading about it – your Everyman of Sport, your Sporting Wanderer if you like, can turn his or her hand, and tongue, to all these. This individual may not be much good on the field of play but is earthily eloquent in describing the feats of others, and as impartial as anybody can be. It matters not to him or her what sport is in question – boxing or bowls, cricket or croquet. Our hero (be it a he or a she, but for convenience sake I shall make him a he) is admirably curious about sport in general, and one takes to him at once. For he is a living denial of that hierarchy of sport, prevalent in the media, which elevates a few games above the many, and then writes those few to death.

There is also a hierarchy within every game. I once met,

at Bristol's ground, a man who was a living denial of that hierarchy in rugby. He told me that he travelled all over the West Country to watch matches. He was not a selector, a journalist, a salesman, or a widower with time on his hands, but simply a man who loved rugby. One Saturday might find him in Redruth, the Wednesday after in Torquay, and the Saturday after that in Exeter. He seemed to have positive views about every team, from Penzance-Newlyn in the west to Cheltenham in the east, and he did not care whether they were first-class or not. Barnstaple versus St Ives and Gloucester versus Cardiff were for him equally worth watching. He told me all this before the kick-off. I happened to meet him again at the bus stop, after the match, and he gave me his impressions. He was concise and comprehensive, and he crystallized one or two points that I used later in my report; a journalist is wise not to be fussy about the table from which his crumbs fall. That man represented a salutary minority. He had no snobbish notions about watching only "the best", and if he had to stand on streaming duckboards at Much-Binding-in-the-Marsh instead of sit at opulent Leicester, it would not occur to him to grumble.

Doubtless he discovered sport as a small boy, for sport is inextricably linked with growing up; indeed, it is almost a metaphor for it. Sport has been the saving of many a youth, and not just in the physical sense. Some boys grow up interested in sport and nothing else. They would not give tuppence for science and arithmetic but they would give a small fortune for soccer and cricket, and soon become fluently knowledgeable in both. Without realizing it at the time, they are making certain that later in life, wherever they are and whoever they are with, they will rarely be at a loss in conversation: for have we not agreed that sport is among the most universal of subjects?

We can often place significant events in our lives in the context of sport. Rugby was the first game I experienced, and I came to it quite late, having carefully avoided organized sport of any kind for most of my boyhood. We had a teacher at the Aberdeen Grammar School, Dallas – "Dally" – Allardice, who played scrum half for Scotland in the 1940s, after an eventful war in the Commandos. I owed my awakening partly to him and partly to my father, an ardent rugby man, who used to tell me about being at the opening of Murrayfield in 1925 to see Scotland complete their first grand slam; he encouraged me to involve myself in at least one of the school's sporting activities, if only out of loyalty.

I was a hopeless player but contrived to enjoy it in the lower reaches, the sixth, seventh and eighth teams, with "Dally" in long-suffering charge on midweek afternoons, nicely blending instruction and encouragement. I can recall being shown by him how to bind with the hooker, but I did not endure as a prop, and soon gravitated to the second row, the natural home, I found, of all incompetent players, since mistakes made in the thick of the scrum can as a rule be covered up. Michael Green has written that the chief characteristic of coarse rugby is that teams are invariably two or three short. Well, we were the coarsest of the coarse at Rubislaw half a century ago, and manpower, or boypower, was not the only thing we were short of.

"Dally" played in a very successful Grammar Former Pupils' team that included Dr Johnny Innes, a centre who captained Scotland, and, on the wing, Doug Smith, another doctor, who managed the Lions in New Zealand in 1971, startling all concerned by correctly forecasting the result of the test series. In later seasons, when the FPs had become an ordinary side, "Dally", their only extraordinary player, was often chosen at stand-off or even at wing forward. He was criticized for being too individualistic, for losing touch with his support, and there was no doubt that at times he thought and moved too quickly for the rest of his team. But as he also, at times, thought and moved too quickly for the opposition, and scores accrued, there was much to forgive.

Around that period, too, the Grammar had a fine school

side, big, fast and skilful, which went through a season of fourteen matches undefeated. Ernie Michie was in it, a lock forward who subsequently played for Scotland and toured South Africa with the 1955 Lions. I have seen a photograph of him, in his kilt, piping the Lions on to the field. Ron Comber, another member of that school pack, was a wing forward who, with the direct-hit approach that earned him the nickname "Bomber", metamorphosed into a three-quarter, once scoring two tries in a Murrayfield trial.

As for me, when I returned from National Service in Germany, I played no more than three seasons, intermittently, in the FPs' third and fourth teams. I never trained – that would have been difficult anyway, as I was working night shift on the local paper by then; I just received my card and turned up, at Rubislaw, Seafield, Hazlehead, Bridge of Don barracks, or the point of departure for the coach to Lossiemouth, Dundee, Arbroath, or wherever.

Cricket, too, has had a long innings in my affections. I played and umpired a little, and read much, ultimately deciding that Neville Cardus's two autobiographical volumes bound into one could not be bettered as my desert-island book. We were given a half-day holiday from school to watch the Australians playing Scotland at Mannofield in 1948, but that slightly predated the beginning of my interest in the game, and I missed seeing the final century of Bradman's career. In the fifties, Rohan Kanhai was Aberdeenshire's professional, guaranteeing a full house at every match, and I saw hours of him.

When I went to *The Times*, which was then in Queen Victoria Street, and still carried small ads on the front page, I covered county cricket during my holidays. I watched Fred Trueman hit a century off Middlesex at Scarborough; and that rare experience was followed by another at Trent Bridge, where a drawn match between Nottinghamshire and Hampshire ended with the scores tied, the late finish causing me to miss the last train to London.

In the office I handled the copy of some notable writers on the game: A. A. Thomson, Denzil Batchelor, John Arlott (under the pen-name John Silchester), Jack Fingleton, Alan Gibson, and, of course, the paper's own John Woodcock. Gibson once informed his readers that he had written his report of the day's play in a church pew. One of Thomson's many books is called *Pavilioned in Splendour*, a title to which a pious aunt of mine took exception because the phrase comes from a hymn. I recall speaking to Batchelor when he rang to apologize, in a charming way, for some trivial error in his piece a day or so before. Three weeks later I read of his death.

This book ends on the bowling green, which is a good place to end, for the game now preoccupies me, as business or pleasure, often both, all the year round. Big money and rampant self-aggrandizement have not yet spoiled it, as they have spoiled some other games. It is the only sport at which I have persevered as a player, and I took it up, over twenty years ago, on a whim – which is perhaps the best way of taking up anything in life.

2
A Sort of Sporting Buddhist

A haunting tale

I have never seen a ghost and I have met only one ghost
writer. He made a living out of writing sportsmen's books
for them. He had no need to do anything else; any sportsman
– or sportswoman – who was anybody approached him first
when they wanted to become authors with an autobiography
or instructional book. They almost queued for his services.

I know that if I had been a sportsman and wanted my life
embalmed in print, I would have placed the task in this man's
hands with complete confidence. He was a fine upstanding
figure, not at all like a ghost, with perfect discretion, a
detached charm, and even, from my limited reading of his
works, some ability to write. I shall call him Herbert. That
was not his name, but I have to respect his professional wish
for anonymity.

He once told me the story of his life, which must have made

a welcome change from telling the stories of other, perhaps lesser, men's lives. Up to a point it was a story lacking in detail. So little did Herbert give away that I might have been listening to a secret agent under interrogation. But then a ghost writer is a species of secret agent, with an anorak for a cloak, a typewriter instead of a dagger, the simplest of codes, and in Herbert's case, it seemed, a minimal private life.

Herbert was born in —— (here he mentioned a seaside resort, adding that he trusted me to keep the fact to myself). His parents, now dead, had been middle-class and unambitious. He had a brother and a sister, with both of whom he had lost touch – probably, I conjectured, at his insistence.

He went to grammar school and university but declined to say which. "Not Oxbridge," he confided, in a rush of information. Then came the army. "I admit I hoped for the Education Corps," he said, "but they put me in the —— instead." Again, he swore me to secrecy concerning the identity of what he termed his 'mob'. However, I do not think I am lifting too much of the veil if I say that I gathered, from hints, that he served at Aldershot and in the Middle East.

On demobilization he could not decide what to do. He had a degree in Oriental studies – this he told me almost in a whisper – but no employer seemed interested. Eventually, after odd jobs, he drifted on to a local paper "somewhere in the north of England," reported council meetings, weddings, flower shows and pigeon racing for a year or two, and then tiptoed into Fleet Street.

Was that when the ghost-writing began? "Yes and no," he replied in his inimitably precise way. "You see, this sportsmen's agent got me into a corner at a party in Pimlico. He was looking rather urgently for someone to do a short book which the latest England striker could attach his name to, and of course from there one thing led to another. It all happened quite by chance."

I discovered to my astonishment that Herbert had never

played any sport. "Laziness pure and simple," he explained. "I've never watched much sport, either. I thought it tedious just to stand there gaping and probably catching cold or having beer poured over me.

"But writing the life histories of all these players – that's different. Fascinating. It's like acting, really. I've got to learn a new part with every new book. I've got to think myself under the players' skins and into their minds – when they have one. I've got to *be* them.

"In fact, it occurs to me that every time I write a book, I may lose a little more of my own identity. But I don't mind. I don't even mind when the players go to Hatchards to sign copies of books that I wrote.

"I consider myself a sort of sporting Buddhist. The Buddhist looks forward to various reincarnations. Well, I have to reincarnate myself over and over again. This year I might be a footballer, next year a cricketer, the year after that an athlete, and so on. And I look forward to them all.

"It's a pity but people don't see my job in that light. They think it's hack work, scissors and paste, a tape-recorder job, with little skill and less imagination. But it needn't be, if you take pains and do it well."

And the players themselves? "Most of them are all right. A few are slobs. But I can't afford to be too choosy. Even if some superstar comes along that I wouldn't feed to the dog, I have to be as pleasant and cooperative as I can. Anyway, when relations get strained, I say to myself: the pen is mightier than the racket.

"The goals and runs I've scored! Why, by the time I pack up, I reckon I'll have lived the life of just about every kind of top sportsman you can imagine, if you see what I mean – and without all the tiresome effort. I'm a true all-rounder, in fact. I'm proud of that."

Before we parted, he asked me how I had become interested in ghost writers. I said that many moons ago I used to walk home from work in the early morning with a sub-editor who believed that Bacon wrote Shakespeare's plays. Herbert laughed and said he believed that, too.

Before the battle

The name George Washington staring out at me from an article about women's tennis is a reminder of the uneasy part played by popular history in sports journalism. I have often been picked up in the middle of reading a piece on some blameless pastime and deposited among the legs of the charging Light Brigade or at the bottom of a shell crater at Passchendaele.

The Duke of Wellington has much to answer for. Not only did he defeat Napoleon at Waterloo, but he is also supposed to have said that the battle was won on the playing fields of Eton. He described it as "a damned nice thing – the nearest run thing you ever saw in your life", which ever since, in newspaper accounts of a myriad sporting contests, has been garbled into "a close run thing".

Henry V exhorting his army before Agincourt is a convenient image for a captain motivating the lads in the dressing room, and Drake ignoring the Armada and stooping to finish his game of bowls will serve for any ice-cool English sportsman in a crisis. When "the Gatling's jammed and the Colonel dead" in Newbolt's poem, a schoolboy rallies the ranks in the desert with his cry of "Play up! play up! and play the game!'

This is all harmless enough. Not so harmless, to anyone with a sense of the ridiculous, is the practice of dragging historical figures from the past into the present, giving them front seats at traditional sporting occasions, and speculating as to how they might react. Thus we might read that "if the Iron Duke" (I said Wellington has a lot to answer for) "had been at Twickenham, he would have nodded in approval at the fighting spirit of England's gallant forwards", that "England's last-wicket pair defied Australia with a determination which would have gladdened Monty's heart", or that "had Colonel Cody, better known as Buffalo Bill, been at Hickstead, he would have applauded the way David Broome handled a difficult horse during his clear round."

Marshals, generals, colonels – you cannot avoid the military on a subject like this; and, of course, sporting events can be seen, all too obviously, as battles. We have already had Passchendaele (Ivan Vodanovich, the All Blacks coach, made an inflammatory reference to it during the Lions tour of 1971), Waterloo and Agincourt, and to a certain type of imagination every Scottish victory is a Bannockburn and every Scottish defeat a Flodden. There are teams who meet their Waterloo, either in Belgium or at Blundellsands, and retreats from Moscow, when some football club or other lose in Russia, are frequent.

On a smaller scale are showdowns and shootouts, deriving from the American West, legend or fact as the case may be. High noon has passed into the vocabulary of sport and become a cliché. I myself have used Jesse James and Dodge City.

I have also used George Orwell, who said that sport is war minus the shooting – which leads me to a final and by no means irrelevant digression. Like generals and battles, authors are useful for leavening the lump of daily journalism. I know that quotations from them may be no more than proof of a retentive memory, but the trumpet-note of a different voice cutting through the journalese can reawaken the reader's interest.

In my time I can remember quoting a mixed bag of Shaw, Saki, Dylan Thomas, Wodehouse, Cardus and Noel Coward, but never Shakespeare. Elizabethan English is a dead language to me. So Henry V has never addressed any of my teams before the battle. I fear he might have confused them.

Raining supreme

With one of those blinding strokes of originality that occur to me every twenty-five years or so, I am going to discuss the weather. No, I am not going to try to upstage the people in High Holborn, although I am as capable as they are of forecasting a changeable day. I am thinking of the weather as it affects sport.

George Gissing wrote that "For the man sound in body and serene of mind there is no such thing as bad weather." There spoke the idealist. You can understand his view, if you cannot quite share it. But if you are a cricketer or cricket watcher there can be no qualifying "quite" about it. Your sympathy with Gissing is non-existent. Bad weather means no play, and that is a catastrophe.

For students of the weather there is no game to compare with cricket. In general terms, a beautiful day makes dull batting endurable. You can always sun yourself, sleep, or read about what happened yesterday. But if it is not warm, and the cricket is pedestrian, you feel cheated and wish yourself elsewhere, as if you had gone to the theatre believing the play to be powerful, and found it flat.

In particular terms, the weather suggests the course and result of the match, be it only another draw. The older breed of cricket reporters like to work in early a few statements such as, "It was a fine morning, but cloudy in the afternoon," and,

Despite a broken arm, Colin Cowdrey goes out to bat in fading light during the dramatic last over of the England–West Indies Test match at Lord's in 1963. (Photograph: Sport & General)

"Rain is likely to make the wicket turn." They have a sure grasp of essentials: the weather first, and then the score, since one conditions the other.

I remember snow stopping play in June – it was at Buxton in 1975. I remember a Test match between England and West Indies at Lord's, less for its famously close finish than for John Arlott's summing-up of the day's play, closing with the words, "And then the lightning flashed and the thunder rolled and the rain came and washed it all away."

Neville Cardus once ended a report by praising the hardihood and dedication of two spectators at a county match at Leicester who sat huddled beside the sightscreen all day in spite of a cold wind. "But perhaps," he wrote as an afterthought, "they were only dead."

On the whole I think the weather useful decoration. A little meteorological word-spinning may breathe life into the account of some event doomed to be forgotten as soon as over. Years ago I saw the evening sky above the Arsenal ground described as "Turneresque," and the fact that I have remembered the image and forgotten the result of the match perhaps proves my point.

What is not decorative, but nonsensical, is the use of the weather as a person. "The sun came out in the second half in time to inspire a Harlequins revival." "The heavens wept over the downfall of Real Madrid." "The moon hid behind a cloud in shame at the disgraceful scenes on the terraces." Walt Disney "humanized" animals in a similar manner, but he had some biological justification. In contrast the weather is as impersonal as a stone.

Tennis, like cricket, is a delicate plant. One shower and the courts empty. Scarcely a year passes but the first day of Wimbledon is not marked by suggestive photographs of spectators staring at puddles in SW19.

They have problems indoors, too. In the small print recently appeared the information that there had been no play in an indoor tennis championship because of rain. Please do not rush to dismiss this as an example of dry humour. It could have been poor workmanship by the builders.

No interest in marbles

One of the little hardships of being a sports journalist is that people expect you to have tickets for every event under the sun. Only the other day I happened to mention my job to a casual acquaintance, who promptly asked if I could get him two tickets for the world marbles championship in Bangkok, or wherever it was. I replied that I was not into marbles, which seemed to surprise him.

That was an easy one to answer. But my stock response is to assure the inquirer that if I had a hundred tickets he would be welcome to the lot. My reason is not generosity but the fact that I am usually asked for tickets for events I would pay to keep away from, those, as a rule, being the events for which the bulk of the population would go to any length short of murder to obtain a seat.

I, too, have gone to certain lengths in the distant past, when sport was not my business. Once I bought a black market ticket outside Twickenham for an England-Ireland match and was quite surprised – should I have been? – to be allowed in without the police being summoned.

Another year I went to Wembley to see England play Scotland but at the last moment declined to pay the touts their price and returned early to Baker Street. Before the match the grass verges of the approach road to the stadium were littered with Scots supporters in drunken slumber. They were wiser than they knew, because England won 9–3.

I am in a different position now. If the public are to be believed, I can lay my hands on tickets for everything, everywhere. No longer do I have to rely on luck, or touts, or queueing at the turnstiles. From the Olympic Games and the World Cup to crown green bowls, the whole of sport is supposed to be open to me.

Even if this were true, it would not enthral me. As I said, many are the events I would pay not to see; and at those I do see, which I make sure have at least a semblance of interest for me in the first place, I often feel guilty when I show my press pass and walk in free. It is a vague feeling, hard to explain, possibly rooted in some perverse notion that I am enjoying a privilege I have not earned.

A famous pre-war Welsh international who later became a journalist was once refused admittance to Cardiff Arms Park because he had forgotten his pass and the gateman failed to recognize him. It was like Sir Gordon Richards being refused admittance to Epsom. The famous one was annoyed, partly, perhaps, because his fame cut no ice with a humble official. He had to go home and fetch his pass, like any other hack.

With or without a pass, I have not yet been refused admittance. "Ah, *The Times*," they murmur at the gate, as if repeating the name of some learned society far removed from rucks and loose ball. "See and give us a good write-up."

A lost childhood

Sports reporters should stop referring to the *Boy's Own Paper* when they have to describe some incredible occurrence. It is an insult to the *BOP*, much of which, as I remember it, was quite credible, and a hundred times more thrilling to read than sport. It is also, by extension, an insult to *Chums*, a less well remembered periodical than the *BOP*, but one that I preferred.

My boyhood came too late for the heyday of the *BOP* and *Chums*, but I used to seek out their annuals in second-hand bookshops, and it was, I think, in *Chums* that I first discovered my favourite writer for boys, Charles Gilson. I then read every book of his I could find – and he wrote many, with titles like *The Realm of the Wizard King* and *The Pirate Aeroplane*. I would read a whole book in an afternoon, crouched on the floor, and eating bread and jam. Years afterwards I saw Gilson praised in an essay by Graham Greene called The Lost Childhood. My boy's intuition must have been sound.

At the time of life that I was devouring Gilson's stories I had no interest in sport. That, if you must, was incredible – more incredible, maybe, than anything in the *Boy's Own Paper*, since all boys are stupidly assumed to be mad on sport. Not I, not then. I loathed athletics. Sports afternoons at school were to be avoided if possible. Often I played truant and sneaked off to a cowboy film instead.

The only kind of sport I tolerated was street cricket, with a tree for the stumps. We played on a street that sloped and I scored hundreds of runs by hitting the ball – a tennis ball – downhill, so that the fielder, dodging the traffic as he went, might almost disappear from view among the houses before retrieving it. I took wickets also, and in general showed Test match quality in that form of the game.

But with a real cricket ball I was a coward. It was too hard and dangerous. The nets were my refuge. I could dodge the column there and pass the time unnoticed until escaping to do something useful, such as read Gilson, F. S. Brereton, W. E. Johns, Percy Westerman, and other heroes. They wrote about soldiers and pirates and airmen and explorers. Had they written about footballers and cricketers I would never have opened their books.

Times have changed. I now voluntarily read a fair amount about sport, fact and fiction, the two sometimes indistinguishable. Whether I enjoy it half as much as I enjoyed those old serials in the *Boy's Own Paper* and *Chums*, I very much doubt.

Call me Marker

One of the earliest pen-names I encountered – apart from Sapper, Mark Twain, O Henry and the like – was Jack High. The man who used it was a retired banker who wrote about bowls in a morning paper I worked for, and it was in a sense my initiation into a game that became for me, a quarter of a century later, that envied combination, business and pleasure.

At about the same time that I was editing Jack High's copy (not that it needed much editing, for the banker knew his English as well as his bowls), I was helping out as a racing tipster known as The Colonel. This was my nearest approach to commissioned rank. Not long before, I had spent two years in the Army as a full private, having only once been threatened with promotion to lance-corporal. It was therefore a novel experience to masquerade as a full colonel who knew good horseflesh when he saw it, and doubtless had a distinguished war record.

My knowledge of racing, like my knowledge of the officers' mess, was nil, but I contrived now and then to pick a winner at a decent price, and my interest in the job grew to the point where I would buy an evening paper to discover as early as possible how my selections had run, if at all. Years afterwards,

when I read that The Colonel had won some annual tipsters'
award, I could not help speculating about his likely elevation
to The General.

I like pen-names. There is an old-fashioned ring about them
now, which adds to their potency. Besides being evocative,
they are no less likely to be remembered by newspaper readers
than the real names of correspondents. Did not Cardus make
his early reputation as Cricketer?

If I had to write under pen-names about my two sports,
rugby and bowls, I would choose Second Row and Marker.
Those are not idle choices: there are reasons for both.

The rugby I played was the coarse kind, my customary
position the second row, and after a while I realized that, as
an incompetent player even by coarse standards, I had been
stuck there to get me out of the way. A forward's mistakes are
less glaring and costly than a back's.

Marker is different. In case you do not know the game
of bowls, a marker's basic duties in a singles match are
to place the jack, measure for the shot if necessary,
keep the score, and say nothing unless asked by the
players. Nobody says nothing more eloquently than I
do. I enjoy marking and consider myself good at it. I
would be happy to submerge my identity in the pen-name
Marker.

It is not quite the same thing, but the participants in
sport occasionally want to be called something else. At
one hospitals rugby match the referee mentioned that
he was supposed to be at work that afternoon and
asked us not to publish his true name, for fear of the
sack.

"What do you suggest instead?" I asked. "J. Smith (London)?"

"No, no, not Smith or Jones, please. The boss might see
through it. I was thinking of A. Wol."

Slow on the uptake as usual, I looked blank. "A. Wol," I
repeated, with tentative Teutonic pronunciation.

"Yes," the referee said, "AWOL, Absent Without Leave."

One touch of sport

I am a voracious reader of profiles and interviews in newspapers, and if it comes to light that the subject enjoys sport
my opinion of him goes up. An interest in sport makes a man
– or woman – seem human.

From that you can deduce the kind of things, some out-
wardly trivial, that I look for. I do not give one straw, never
mind two, whether a man has been president of the Oxford
Union or president of the United States, and his political
allegiance means no more to me than the fact that he likes
his steaks well done.

I skip these minor concerns and get down as quickly as
possible to the second half of the article, where in my
experience most of the really revealing information is to be
found – his parentage, what if anything he did at school, his
early ambitions, his first job, where he fought in the war,
whether he has a wife, his domestic habits, clues to his
temperament, books written, musical preferences, pets kept,
general prejudices, peculiarities and pastimes. Of pastimes
in the sporting sense there may be none, in which case I
will finish the article feeling disappointed. He may even
put me off him completely by saying that he loathes sport
and gets his exercise from gardening, an activity that leaves
me unmoved.

But if he mentions that he once played for Shrewsbury Town
reserves, or always has eighteen holes at Gleneagles when
he is up in that direction, or solves his business problems
over a game of billiards, or never misses an international
at Twickenham, then he has me on his side straightaway,
whatever his other failings.

Sir Alfred Ayer is a philosopher, but he is also a follower

of Tottenham Hotspur, which is a fact more likely to make you warm to him than his philosophy. And who can tell how much his philosophy has been helped by his observation of Tottenham over the years? Why, if he had followed some team like Hartlepool United or Crewe Alexandra, he might have been granted even profounder insights.

Harold Pinter's plays have puzzled a few people but there is nothing obscure about his devotion to cricket. And just as following Tottenham may have influenced Ayer's speculations, so the mysteries of spin bowling may have sent Pinter along devious ways in dialogue.

I would also be encouraged to learn that a footballer was into philosophy or a cricketer into modern drama, but that is beside the point here, which is that one touch of sport can make the whole world kin.

Anatomy of a scribe

The day is coming when sports journalists will need medical qualifications to do their work. Picture the scene in the editor's room. Enter a keen young, green young man who wants, in his own words, to "break into" sports journalism, as if it were Buckingham Palace.

Passing quickly over minor matters such as the aspirant's ability to write good English or the extent of his sporting knowledge, the editor becomes serious and, leaning forward in his chair, puts to him a number of forensic questions, of which the following might be taken as typical:
What is a haematoma?
Where is the cervical vertebra?

How would you treat a carbuncle?

What would you prescribe for food poisoning?

In an emergency would you be able to insert a few stitches?

If you were reporting women's sport could you, if suddenly called on, deliver a baby?

To be sure of getting the job the young man would need to answer at least four of these questions correctly. Anything less and the editor would send him back to the *Illustrated Family Doctor*, like a failed learner-driver to the Highway Code.

Why? Because sport, more so now than it has ever been if the public prints are to be believed, is as much about not playing because you are one degree under as it is about playing because you are a super-fit superstar. "Fitness fights" are headlined daily, even though the unfit person is in no condition to fight anything or anybody, confined to bed, as he may well be, with one leg suspended in mid-air or a temperature going through the roof.

The other day I read about a footballer who could not play in a cup tie because he had "collected a strain in the reserves." This news left me hoping and praying that I never have a strain in my reserves. It sounds a sinister as well as painful complaint, and certainly not one I would go out of my way to "collect."

How, in fact, do you "collect" a strain? Is there a supermarket, a sort of central takeaway, where you can go and ask for such things? I would imagine it to be a huge place, about twice the size of Selfridges, with departments supplying all needs: in short, something for the whole family of happy hypochondriacs in sport.

For there seems no limit to the reasons given for So-and-So not being able to chase a ball or whatever he does in that line. Groin strains, pulled hamstrings, blood clots, ankle knocks, cut heads, ingrowing toenails, stomach upsets, bruised shins, detached retinas, broken wrists, ricked backs, dislocated collarbones . . . right down to the common cold, the high season for which will soon be here, along with Christmas, to cheer us all up and keep the sports journalists busy with anxious diagnosis.

Occasionally some part of a sportsman's body becomes national news, almost national property. Remember Denis Compton's knee, Colin Cowdrey's feet, Henry Cooper's eyes, Willie Henderson's toe – the one with the bunion? These were serial stories that ran for weeks. For all I know, people wrote to *The Times* about them. You were ostracized in the best society if you did not know the latest instalment. In the pubs they talked of nothing else, ignoring threats of world war.

The sports journalist must keep his finger on this collective pulse. In his professional capacity he must be able to mix with doctors, physiotherapists, osteopaths and spongemen on equal terms and not be afraid to bandy abstruse words like X-ray and penicillin in casual conversation. He must also be sympathetic to the patients and not give the game away if he happens to know that what is the matter with them is only a scratch.

The case is obvious. Sports journalists need medical qualifications, including a bedside manner, no less than they need typewriters. In-depth journalism being all the rage, it is no use merely saying that a player has an ingrowing toenail and leaving it at that. You must have enough clinical knowledge to take the readers deep into the toenail, to look around it, understand what is going on and feel at home there, like Alice down the rabbit hole. If the keen young, green young man cannot do that he will never win the sports journalist of the year award.

Beige for boredom

A fascinating subject, boredom. Graham Greene once played Russian roulette to stave it off. Most of us do not have that sort of nerve. We play or watch sport instead.

"Bor-ing!" the crowd chant when a team resort too obviously to defensive tactics. "Boring," the dogmatist says of some sport that does not appeal to him; and you can hear the finality in his voice, the ironclad conviction – not the mere opinion – that because he thinks it boring it stands condemned by the whole world. He treats boredom as absolute, when it is only relative.

Hang the world. Anything that does not interest me is boring. That is my definition of boring, and a more questionable definition would be hard to find. It frequently places me in a minority – sometimes, it seems, a minority of one. Sporting events watched by tens of millions from China to Peru have me saying to myself, "Boring, boring," and paying less attention to them than I would to a leaf in the wind.

Yet I can easily be bored by the two sports in which I am most closely involved, rugby and bowls. That is a fact, not a complaint. Such is the contrast between them that you might think boredom impossible, with the relief of turning from one to the other supplying its own stimulus.

Not so, my friends. Rugby matches have sent me to sleep, or would have done if I had not been under a professional obligation to remain awake. At bowls tournaments there have been moments towards the end of a long, warm day when the sight of woods trundling to and fro, to and fro has made me wish never to see another as long as I live.

But in these cases, of course, I always relent and come back for more, not just because it is my job, but because I love the games themselves. Instinctively I see the occasional boredom they inflict on me as part of the process of renewal.

I know a family who dub anybody they consider boring as "beige." It makes a change from grey, at any rate. It is also a less boring, less cult-ridden word than boring. I once went so far as to compose the first paragraph of an imaginary rugby report using beige in that sense. It ran like this:

"A friend of mine tells me that in her family the word beige is commonly used to describe a dull person. At Richmond yesterday I saw a beige match. It was so beige that after a while even the red shirts of one side and the blue of the other seemed to melt and fade into that colour we so often see in cheap wallpaper and dowdy women's coats . . . "

I never used this piece of fancy in a real report, probably because I thought that easily bored people, who are not noted for their imagination, might read no farther.

Money, money, money

"When I was young," Oscar Wilde is supposed to have said, "I thought money was everything. Now that I am older I know it is." Frankly I am tired of money – not of earning it or spending it, but of reading about it, because it has become one of the snobberies of sport.

"Is that all you're offering as first prize – £250,000? Peanuts. Look at us. We're offering £425,000, plus a new car for a hole in one."

And the public swallow it all, believing that more money automatically means more quality and making it clear that, as men and women of the world, they understand the recondite difference between £250,000 and £425,000, not to mention the allure of another car with which to intimidate the neighbours.

The endless talk about big money in sport does not affect me in that way. My only thought is the unoriginal one that I would not mind collecting £250,000 or £425,000, I am not fussy which, for engaging in such ultimately pointless activity. I also have the uneasy feeling that the dustman is a more valuable member of the community than the sportsman waving the cheque with one hand and opening the door of his new car with the other. But that, too, is a form of snobbery.

Another professional sportsman I think about at odd times is the perennial loser. One of the main objects of sport – is it not? – is to win, and yet here we have a man who may spend his entire career coming in far down the field and yet make a decent living for his family in the process.

How often have I looked at the long list of scores at the conclusion of some American golf tournament and seen, twenty or so strokes behind the winner, the same one or two names, usually British. What a life these men must lead: not affluent, perhaps, but comfortable and pleasant and not racked by ambition. Would that failure, or at any rate lack of success, were as well rewarded in other fields.

Good luck to the perennial losers, I say.

Fame going cheap

Facetiousness, the curse of journalism, has its uses. When I read in a football magazine that one fan's claim to fame was that he had once stood behind Glenn Hoddle's mother-in-law at a Tesco checkout, I began wondering if I could produce a claim to match it.

I once sat beside Leslie Compton, brother of Denis, at an annual dinner, but that does not strike the same ringing note, does it? Nor does the fact that I once recognized Cyril Smith, MP, in Whitehall, although fat people, for no logical reason, are supposed to be funny by definition, and if I want the facetious touch I have only to remark that you do not need to be Sexton Blake to recognize Mr Smith.

I could go on, and will. Let the names drop like plums. I have seen many famous sportsmen and spoken to a few. I have seen the Queen and Winston Churchill, both in open cars. I have shaken hands with Rudolf Serkin, the great pianist, in the Green Room at the Festival Hall, and I have had a letter from John Betjeman. At Berchtesgaden, though I did not rub shoulders with Hitler, I saw the terrace where he used to stand looking out across Europe.

But I am not aware of ever having been next to a famous footballer's mother-in-law in Tesco's. Obviously I have not lived.

Humour is a serious business – too serious to be left to the clowns and the journalists. Laugh as much as you like at the football magazine, there is a message implicit in its nonsense. Fame, it whispers, has never been cheaper. You can get it by advertising cat food, or you can get it by standing behind a superstar's mother-in-law in the supermarket.

If I could say that I once sat opposite George Best's aunt in the train and shared a packet of fruit pastilles with her, it would make my name overnight and win me a personality contest, a cheque three feet wide presented by a disc jockey, a chat-show appearance, and a holiday for two in Majorca, where I would not wish to spend a minute, let alone a fortnight.

But I cannot say it and must therefore remain in obscurity. It is more comfortable there anyway, and, oddly enough, you do not notice the crowds. In future, though, I may make a closer scrutiny of my neighbours in Fine Fare.

Lines for all seasons

Sport is much concerned with lines and angles. There is, first, the humbling fact that the sports journalist spends all his life on the sidelines. He watches and records, and sometimes gets things right. One of the daily choices he has to make is the line, or angle, of his report. Does he give news straight or obliquely? Does he, in the classical manner, put the who, what, where and when in the first paragraph, as Damon Runyon advised, or does he, like a true modern, prefer the why, heavily supported by "quotes"? What's my line? is the big question. As Professor Joad said, it all depends.

There he stands, then, on the sidelines, or touchlines, a helpless, if privileged, onlooker. The field is criss-crossed by lines – goallines, halfway lines, byelines – a geometrician's delight, on which forward lines and backlines do all in their power to ignore the shortest distance between two points, a straight line.

The journalist himself has a line – a byline: if he is abroad he has a dateline. Both are treasured possessions. When he is famous, or notorious, people point him out, as they would a statue or a rare plant. The dateline enables him to talk lightly of the cities he has conquered, not to mention the airlines that conveyed him there.

The match produces a scoreline, which occasionally comes out wrong in the paper – a misfortune to add lines to an ageing face. It has happened to me. Blame it on the telephone lines. I once tried six telephone boxes, one after the other, in the centre of Glasgow, and all had been wrecked.

But the frustration of trying to find a public telephone that works can be as nothing compared with the frustration of trying to dictate the Queen's English – I should say my English, which is at least as good as the Queen's – to the office. The result may be crossed lines.

On top of everything sits the headline. The public pay less heed to headlines than they do to the labels, or lines, in supermarkets, but newspapers continue to keep up the pretence that headlines matter. A headline about a Manchester City match once appeared over my report of an England rugby trial at Leicester, but nobody noticed because the wording was so vague that it could have been attached to almost any sport. I am all for that kind of multi-purpose headline, a stock of which should be kept in every office.

Where's Murango?

The ink was hardly dry on the last platitude about the Los Angeles Olympics before the experts were turning in their hundreds to the next Games in Seoul four years hence. In my opinion, and with due respect to Seoul, there is a case for holding them in Murango.

Where? Well might you ask. Eight years ago, during the Montreal Olympics, many other people were asking the same question, particularly if they were readers of *The Times*, which one morning published a table of medal winners that included this memorable information:

	Gold	Silver	Bronze	Total
Murango	0	0	1	1

I made a beeline for my local travel agent and asked him to arrange a fortnight's holiday for me in Murango. At first he was brisk and confident. "Of course, sir. If you could just wait a moment . . . " There spoke a man with the world at his fingertips. No need for a compass. But mystification gradually set in. "It's odd, but I don't seem able to trace this Murango. Are you quite sure that's the name?"

I assured him that I was sure. I had seen it in black and white in *The Times*, and I gave chapter and verse. "In that case I'll have another go", the man said. "*The Times* can't be wrong, can it?" And once again he disappeared into the unknown.

The queue of cosmopolites behind me was meanwhile growing longer and more restive. I did not care. They were only going to the Bahamas and Capri and Paris and Ilfracombe. Compared with them, I was Columbus or Captain Cook. I was going to Murango.

"I'm afraid I'm still having a bit of trouble locating Murango, sir," the travel agent said when he re-emerged. "People say it's a small world, but it's not really. I don't suppose you'd happen to know what hemisphere it's in?"

I shook my head but remarked that I thought the name seemed to have an African ring.

So it was that at the end of three circumnavigations of the globe, and after following a false scent to Spain, the travel agent discovered Murango. He needed a powerful microscope, for it turned out to be, not a country, nor even a region, but a town, a dot on the map of Kenya, too insignificant to appear in any but the larger atlases.

I did not go to Murango after all. I stayed at home that year when, as it happened, the summer was so hot that I doubted whether Murango itself would have been much hotter.

The Murango line in *The Times*, referring to a boxer, not a country, or the town, slipped through in error. Yet there was a certain aptness about it. Murango *sounds* like an Olympic nation, probably one specializing in long-distance runners. The name could also be used, I think, as the title of a musical – or a farce.

Cheers for wives

It is wrong of me, perhaps, but I never believe successful sportsmen when they glibly say, "I owe it all to her" – meaning the wife. I am also sceptical about successful sportswomen (I decline to call them sportspersons) who say they owe it all to their husbands.

They may owe a little, but not all, and that little is probably very little indeed, amounting to no more than lip-service, an occasional word of encouragement, as easily given as a penny for the Guy.

You will never convince me that a man who has just won the Olympic marathon or the Tour de France, or hit a triple century off the West Indian fast bowlers, is being entirely truthful and sincere when he sags in a chair afterwards and gasps out to a credulous press conference that "I owe it all to Samantha." Samantha is without doubt a jolly fine girl, the sort Betjeman would have admired, but she does not have to train and sweat. She has more important business at home, and quite right too.

Samantha, in any case, has a guilty secret, shared, I suspect, with thousands of wives. She is not interested in sport in the slightest, not even in hockey sticks, jolly or otherwise. She would never let on to her beloved, though, and nods and smiles with charming sympathy when he extols the wonders of track and field to her. Two cheers for Samantha, then, but three for the wives I like most – those who make the tea. They give you no empty phrases; they roll up their sleeves and do something practical, and we owe it all to them that our Saturday afternoons can be so homely and appetising.

To see what I mean, go along to some rugby grounds, say Rosslyn Park and Saracens, where, before and after the game, you will find the womenfolk (personfolk) serving sandwiches, pies, pasties, sausage rolls, cakes, tarts, scones and biscuits in a cheerful clatter of efficiency. It always looks to me like a labour of love, and it prompts me to ask a topical question; now that women have started playing rugby, will their husbands rush to serve behind the counter?

I have to confess that it is not unknown for me to base my written estimate of a match on whether I enjoyed the food there. If it was tasty, I might be kind to a bad match, but if it was stodgy – a rare happening – I could be unkind to a good one. Maybe the press, like an army, marches on its stomach.

Age doesn't count

I have no curiosity about sportsmen's ages. When I see a wing three-quarter score a brilliant try I do not rush round to the dressing-room afterwards, burst in without knocking and ask him how old he is.

I am happy to assume, unless there is convincing evidence to the contrary, that he is between eighteen and thirty, give or take a year or two, and even happier to go in lifelong ignorance of his birthday, because that saves me the trouble and expense of sending him a card.

All this, and not only this, consigns me to a minority among journalists. The sports pages are crammed with twenty-two-year-old strikers, seventeen-year-old apprentice jockeys, twenty-five-year-old heavyweight boxers, thirty-eight-year-old veteran spinners and, in the "quality" press, men like Joe Soap, aged twenty-nine, who won the gold medal for clay pigeon shooting. It makes me feel old to read it – and I have to think twice to remember my own age.

Nor does it end there. In certain sports there seems to be a passion for publicizing not only the gentleman's age but also his occupation. By turning to the back of your paper you can make the acquaintance of, perhaps, a fifty-one-year-old boot and shoe tycoon who owns racehorses, a forty-four-year-old unemployed chimney sweep who plays bowls, or a twenty-three-year-old hair stylist who has found there is more money in snooker. I once came across, in a horse-racing report, a middle-aged former leader of the Vienna Philharmonic Orchestra. Where else could you move in such high society?

Many years ago I worked for the *Daily Telegraph* and one of its multifarious editorial rules was that you had to state the tonnage of every ship mentioned in its columns. This was liable to have curious results. For example: "Miss Elizabeth Taylor, the actress, arrived at Southampton from New York yesterday on board the liner Queen Mary (80,000 tons)."

Giving sportsmen's ages seems to me in most cases to be as pointless as giving the tonnages of ships. Was Miss Taylor's arrival made more interesting or significant by the fact that she had 80,000 of Cunard's luxurious tons beneath her? Does it matter that the wing three-quarter who scored the winning try blew out twenty-four candles last Sunday? There is every reason to believe he would have scored it whether he had been twenty or twenty-eight and born in a leap year or on April Fool's Day.

If a fifteen-year-old schoolboy or a sixty-six-year-old semi-retired piano tuner breaks a world record, or does something else outstanding, you cannot avoid giving his age. The extremes are newsworthy. Otherwise a sportsman's age is of no more importance than the colour of his eyes – and the dynamic reporter, anxious to prove his powers of observation, drags in even that sometimes: "The sinuous, black-eyed, phenomenally gifted, nineteen-year-old goalscoring prodigy and national hero with the pop-star image from the back streets of Rio . . . "

Rude voices

Imagine yourself a civilian in the middle of a war – I mean a real war, not a skirmish between football supporters. Imagine a stranger stopping you to ask what you thought of it. Pausing only to dodge a hail of bullets, would you give him a considered answer or tell him, in words of one syllable, what to do?

The stranger is a newspaper correspondent looking for so-called human interest. He has listened to the generals (as though they were not human); now he wants the common man's opinion. I do not habitually read war dispatches but in most of those I have read there was comment, possibly authentic, from unidentified bystanders – a man at a bus stop, a woman in a shop, a mother in the rubble of her home – and it occurs to me that we could do with some of that savour in the closed world of sport.

We have had too much of what the players think. The people who never get a hearing are the public, the customers, who keep the players in business and are supposed to be always right. I am not saying that their comments would necessarily be better than those of the players. But in most cases they could not be worse, which is a basis for optimism.

Imagine yourself, therefore, a spectator leaving the ground at the end of a football match. A breathless young man in a duffel coat introduces himself to you as a reporter. You look suspiciously at his biro. He asks what you thought of the game. Imagine your possible replies in all their lurid variety: "Never seen such a load of old rubbish." "Whole team ought to be sacked." "Relegation's too good for them." "Worst manager this club's ever had." "Why didn't I stay at home and watch the darts?" "Take it from me, the missus had a more exciting afternoon in Tesco's." "It's the end of football as far as I'm concerned." And so forth in the same vein.

Nothing lurid about that language, I agree, but you must realize I have had reluctantly to censor certain popular adjectives. Even so, you still get the unmistakable impression that the match was not worth crossing the street to see: which makes a contrast with the bland statements of the obvious by players and managers.

It depends what you want to read – the thousand-times-repeated junk such as "We didn't put it all together and take our chances" or the colloquial honesty of "The missus had a more exciting afternoon in Tesco's" (not forgetting the adjectives). I know which I prefer.

Don't believe doctors

Are you worried about your health? Are you frightened of dying young – say at seventy-five? If so, I would advise you not to read newspapers.

This is not in the least because they are full of matters like nuclear warfare and dangerous diseases, over most of which we have no control. It is because they are full of grave assurances by doctors and quacks of all sorts that we are unfit, that we are a naughty nation of lazy boys and girls, and that if we do not mend our ways we are doomed.

I feel sorry for the many people who believe every word of it. What miserable lives they must lead, endlessly worried about their future, like poor Benjamin in *The Graduate*.

They are worried about not taking enough exercise; about taking too much; above taking none at all; about drinking or not drinking; about whether to stop smoking at once or gradually; about diets, calories, carbohydrates, cholesterol; about heart attacks; about watching too much television; about driving the car when they ought to be driving a golf ball; about feelings of guilt aroused by the sight of joggers; about the best sport to take up – should they try squash or stick to frisbees?

I am sorry for these people, nervous wrecks to the last man and woman, because they should know better than to believe everything they read, particularly the long words. If they were less worried they would notice that the doctors contradict each other. One week they recommend jogging; the next, warn against it. On Monday butter is bad for you. Come Friday it is good. First it is moderation in all things. Then it is do as you please.

The doctors make a study in themselves. Where do they

all come from with their babel? Who solicits their generali-
zations? What do they do in their spare time – apart, that
is, from grunt and sweat in the gymnasium? Most of them
seem to live and work where nobody can get hold of them
and tell them to stop. Their reports, as far as the man in the
Clapham omnibus is concerned, might as well emanate from
Tibet – although that may be the general idea, to speak like
royalty from such a height and distance that the awestruck
populace can only bow and accept.

Their reports would be more valuable if there were far fewer
of them. It is useful to be reminded occasionally, in an age
of passive entertainment and fast food, of the importance of
treating your body with respect. It is useless to be reminded
every week, almost, and in conflicting terms.

Between you and me, I think it all comes down in the end
to heredity and luck, which are factors rarely mentioned. If
your parents were healthy, you have a good chance of being
healthy, too. Mine were, and I have had scarcely a day's illness
in fifty years.

That is not to say that I will not have to be rushed into inten-
sive care next week. But it seems unlikely. In the meantime,
I shall continue to live abstemiously, eat what suits me, take
plenty of congenial exercise – and turn a blind eye to the latest
report warning me that I am doing a hundred things wrong
and must change my habits or die.

Telly gets tedious

A doleful Australian comedian called Bill Kerr used to end
his act on radio by singing a song with the refrain, "Life Gets

Tedious, Don't It?" Sport gets tedious, too, and for that reason I want to go off at a tangent to another of the world's pet subjects – television.

I know that is the easy option but I cannot resist it because, when I compare myself with those who write about television for a living, I realize that I have one huge advantage over them: I watch the box very little. It is an advantage not to be wasted.

Besides, any hack worth his typewriter ribbon knows that one touch of television makes the whole world kin and that a sure way of getting a response to his work is to write disrespectfully of television. I can prove it. I received eight letters about a recent piece in which I said I did not watch a single minute of the Olympic Games last summer, and that is eight more than usual.

Five of the letters were sympathetic, two were sceptical, and one was abusive. I relished the abusive letter no less than the others, since you always stand to learn more from blame than from praise. If memory serves me right, it accused me of crassness and inconsistency and implied that people like me are responsible for the decadence of Western society – or something along those lines.

As far as I can judge viewing habits in general – and I have had some miserable experiences in other people's houses – it would seem that the majority look up the programmes in the paper, then switch on the set as a matter of routine, and leave it on for hours, whether or not anyone is watching. There is little or no conscious process of selection. They might as well not look in the paper, for all its apparent influence on them.

When I have an evening at home, I, too, look up the programmes in the paper, on the off-chance that there might be an item worth watching, but nineteen times out of twenty I think to myself, "What a feeble lot", and do something else. This may be evidence that my range of interests is narrow, but I naturally prefer to believe it shows my sound instinct for recognizing rubbish a mile off.

Just as I am proud of not having watched the Olympics, so I am proud of never having watched *Dallas* or any other soap opera. From the sound of them – and who am I to doubt the analytical powers of the critics? – they are too clever and sophisticated for me. I prefer simple little programmes like *One Man and His Dog* and *Face the Music* – in the one case because Border collies are superior to actors, and in the other because I can sometimes beat the panel at their own game.

There is, as you know, a strong competitive or sporting element in both programmes, whether you are counting sheep trotting through a gate or trying to identify Sibelius played backwards. But it is not the only element. *One Man and His Dog* would be nothing without its hills and skies. In the same way, I have heard non-golfers say they enjoy watching golf on television because of the scenery at seaside links.

I regard television as an occasional, strictly controlled pastime, not as a habit. The only time I watched it at breakfast was in 1983, when the British Lions were playing the All Blacks, and it put me off my boiled egg. On the one or two occasions I have watched it at midnight I invariably woke up next morning with a headache.

No, television, for me, belongs, like sport itself, to certain times of the day, neither early nor late. I am a creature of habit, but not of the viewing habit. Television can get tedious much quicker than life or sport.

Acronyms, please

I know what NATO and ACAS mean but until the other day, when I chanced to dip into a new magazine called

Everywoman, I did not know that WASH means Women
Against Sexual Harassment.

Sport needs a few acronyms like that to brighten it up. FIFA
and UEFA are the only ones that occur to me, offhand, and
they are uninspiring. So I thought I would concoct a few which
might come in useful. I like to make constructive suggestions
occasionally and belie the journalist's reputation as a cynical
"knocker".

Talking of "knocking", why not start with an organization
called RAUC? RAUC should be set up at once. RAUC would
be a boon to a fine but much abused body of men. RAUC, in
case you have not guessed, stands for Referees Against Unfair
Criticism, which is an apt title because criticism of referees, on
the terraces and in the press, is nothing if not raucous.

Two other ideas of mine are almost interchangeable. They
are CASH and SNOSH, and their similarity does not end with
the fact that both sound like sneezes. They are also painfully
topical. Got it, or them? Of course you have, you clever people.
They stand for Campaign Against Soccer Hooliganism and
Stop Nights of Shame.

I happen to think there is no solution to the hooliganism
problem, although I grant that may be the sceptic's instinc-
tive reaction against the hundred and one solutions already
advanced. But nobody can deny that CASH and/or SNOSH
are needed. They might do little more than preserve a window
or a seat here and there but, as my mother used to say, that is
better than a poke in the eye with a sharp stick.

If you have read this far you may be dismissing it as a lot
of hot air. That leads me – thank you very much – to my next
suggestion: GAS. There is a lot of it about. As I have observed
before, we live in the age of the interview, and must pay the
price. One way to reduce the price, so to speak, is to get GAS
going.

It means Gag All Sportsmen. I do not mean that literally or
completely. What I do mean is that GAS might save us from
countless column inches of banality, see to it that pointless

"quotes" are replaced by valuable information, and make the good "quote" earn its space when it comes along – which is about twice a year. I might even offer to serve as chairman of GAS. Being a man of few words I would at least set a good example.

I recently counted thirty-three mentions of the sponsors in a rugby match programme. COST – Control of Sponsorship Tribunal – would ensure that such excesses never happened again and stipulate six mentions as a reasonable maximum. A society for the prevention of cruelty to the English language is also overdue, but I am unable to think of a sufficiently acid acronym.

The lonely sponsor

A well-known construction company sponsor boxing and real tennis. These are not sports you immediately associate with cranes and bulldozers but then sponsorship is a curious business, or industry, liable to pop up in unexpected places.

I have no idea what goes on behind the scenes. How did that company choose boxing and real tennis, which seem mutually exclusive? Did they approach the sports or did the sports approach them? Was it chance? Why not wrestling and archery, or swimming and clay pigeon shooting? Why not hurling, since many Irishmen are supposed to work on building sites?

Consider the sponsors in the two sports that concern me. In rugby you have tobacco and electrics; in bowls you have a building society, a bank, insurance, cameras, stationery and tobacco. Truly there is something for the whole family in

sponsorship. And since family suggests children, I would like
to ask a question that seems to me to define in a subtle way the
entire concept of sponsorship: when is maternity wear going
to pour money into karate?

So far I have been talking about people who are either
happily sponsoring or happily being sponsored. No problem,
as they would say. I come now to those unhappy ones
who have a very big problem indeed: they are either
sponsorless, when they desperately want a sponsor, or
have nothing to sponsor, which makes them feel left on the
shelf.

I am more interested in the second group because I
know an able businessman in that predicament and a
pitiable case he is. For years he has been seeking a
sport to sponsor but in vain. He refuses to sponsor
any sport just for the sake of it. Others do that. He
has a sense of the fitness of things and thinks a sport
and its sponsor should be suited, like a husband and
wife, and mentionable in the same breath without a
giggle.

The difficulty is that his firm manufacture vacuum cleaners
and he has been heard to remark that if you can tell him
of a sport with an instant, clear and logical affinity with
vacuum cleaners your name must be Gunga Din. Jokes
about cleaning up certain sports get a dusty answer.
Another sad point is that he was a keen games player
in his day and yet all his attempts to repay sport for
the pleasure it once gave him are frustrated by the idiotic
fact that he went in for vacuum cleaners instead of string
vests.

Whenever I go to a sponsors' press conference now I think
of my vacuum cleaner tycoon. As I sip pineapple juice and
nibble sausages on sticks it is him that I see, in my mind's eye,
on the other side of the gleaming mahogany table, chatting to
the president of the sport's governing body. Wish you were
here, I think.

All we want is style

I hesitate to raise the subject of sponsors again. They get enough publicity as it is. But you cannot avoid them for long – to adapt a saying of my father's, you can hardly fall out of a window without landing on a sponsor – and, in any case, you have to admit they do a lot of good in sport.

I wrote this article with a pen presented to me by a sponsor, and I look forward to the day when I will be able to say that I typed its successors with a typewriter presented by a sponsor. At the moment, as far as I am aware from limited experience, sponsors do not hand out bulky and expensive equipment to the gentlemen of the press. They give us things like pens and ties and notebooks and leather cases, usually at elegant functions where they ply us also with food and drink and information.

When I say they, I mean some of them. Not all sponsors are generous and helpful. A few would be invisible if they did not have their names added to whatever they sponsor. They keep the press less at arm's length than at bargepole's length. But in the main sponsors are friendly people who do their best to understand a newspaperman's simple needs.

That brings me to a suggestion I want to make to sponsors in general. I hinted at it when I said that I looked forward to typing my articles with a machine given me by a sponsor. Briefly, and to be perfectly honest and brutally frank and unashamedly materialistic; and, further, not to beat around the bush, I would like sponsors to be twice – no, fifty times – as lavish as they are now.

Pens and ties and notebooks are all right in their way, but it is a small way. As is well known, we in the fourth estate value style beyond almost any other quality, and we wish to point out that although pens and ties are useful, and we are grateful for them, they lack style as we conceive it. It is not a question of size alone. It is a question of – how shall I express it? – well, style. There is no other word.

No more ties and pens, then. Journalists could stock a shop with those. Besides, we often get them, along with handkerchiefs, at birthdays and Christmas, when our loved ones cannot think of anything else for presents. What we would like sponsors to do with their spare thousands is to give us clothes and cars and houses. On those terms we would count it a privilege to turn ourselves into perambulating advertisements for sponsors.

I for one can see myself tailored from head to toe by nice sponsors, and provided by them with a flat in town and a house in the country, and a chauffeur-driven car, not only to travel between the two, but also to take me to sporting events. The tailoring would include everything, even socks; the flat and the house would be fully furnished; and the car a model of my own choice, big enough, like that of the old-fashioned girl in Eartha Kitt's song, to have a bowling alley in the back. I do not consider this too much to ask.

A sporting Booker

There ought to be a prize, similar in repute to the Booker, for sports books (I nearly wrote "as prestigious as the Booker" – how easily that slimy adjective slips out). I know the Booker is for fiction, but as any journalist will confirm, some sports reportage is fiction: few in my trade have not written a report and then received a sarcastic letter from a spectator asking whether they had been at the same match.

Not only from spectators. I was once taken to task for writing that a pass given by a certain centre was intercepted by the opposition, who scored a try. The centre wrote to me saying it was not his pass. That was an occasion when I wrote fiction and if it were possible to examine and dissect all sports journalism, you would find enough such lapses to fill books. But back to the Booker for sports books. I was set thinking about it by my own library. It is not large, because only two or three sports interest me and the rest can go hang, but it contains several books that would, I think, have been runaway winners of that hypothetical prize.

Most of Cardus is there and his *Good Days* and *Days in the Sun* would have won it by an innings. I used to have *The Greatest Test of All*, by Jack Fingleton, an account of the 1960 tied match between Australia and West Indies in Brisbane, but it was lent, unknown to me, and never returned. It is not a long book, but prize-worthy, for Fingleton's individual voice comes through, as it did in everything he wrote, and that is what rescues journalism from itself.

The author's voice is even louder and clearer in my favourite rugby tour book, Terry McLean's *Willie Away*. "Willie" was Wilson Whineray, captain of the 1963-64 All Blacks in Britain, and "Willie away" a lineout signal. I reread it recently and it seemed better than ever. I also reread what Chris Laidlaw wrote about it, and about tour books in general, in 1973, in his own *Mud In Your Eye*:

"Terry McLean's books, with perhaps two exceptions, are masterpieces in their own right, not mere chronicles like all the others. His *Willie Away* is clearly the best of these, a pioneering work in the subtle art of player-to-match writing. By assigning his pen portraiture in a match-by-match sequence, McLean gave the tour book a new cohesion and balance."

Those All Blacks lost their chance of a grand slam when they drew 0–0 with Scotland, a match I saw. The player picked out by McLean for pen portraiture was Young, the All Blacks hooker – the "Dad" of the chapter heading – who made five heels against the head, including one on his own line when Scotland seemed bound to score.

The grand slam, McLean began by saying, lay at the end of the rainbow; when the match was over he achieved this dying fall:

"Then Murrayfield gathered itself into darkness and the wispy rainbow faded, leaving only the memory of the might-have-beens to be talked of, winter and summer, until even it, too, faded and was gone."

"Who are the Beatles?"

I have a soft spot for the judge who asked that question during a case at the height of the Beatles era. He may have known who they were, and asked the question for the sake of a titter in court. I prefer to give him the benefit of the doubt and assume that he honestly did not know of their existence. It is, you see, the sort of question I ask. I like sport without being fanatical about it. Hence my habit, when some new sporting superman comes along and sets the nation talking, of inquiring who he is.

"You mean to say you haven't heard of him?" is the incredulous response.

"No," say I.

"But he's all over the newspapers, and on the telly."

"Is he?"

"Of course he is, What's the matter with you, mate? You're supposed to be an expert on sport.

"Hm. Sorry."

End of dialogue. Sometimes, I admit, I play the ignoramus

for a joke. But at other times I have not heard of the superman or know only his name and nothing of the reasons for his celebrity.

I can never, for example, keep up with the turnover in the England football team. It is such as to make me wonder if every player in the first division is an international. I am not so behind the times that I think Bobby Charlton is still playing, but where people like – well, you can fill in the names – are concerned, I could easily drop a clanger.

The trouble, as always, is that the trumpeted supermen are not supermen but mediocrities, and it is in the nature of mediocrities to look the same: which is why they come and go so frequently and why I cannot remember them, any more than I can remember the dozens of people I pass in the street every day. I remember Bobby Charlton, who played years ago, but not Wotsisname, who played last week.

What I say about supermen applies also to superwomen, or superpersons. It was a while before I knew exactly who Zola Budd was, although her picturesque name ought to have been enough to arouse my curiosity, and Nadia Comaneci was almost a figure from the past before I learnt – probably by accident – why everybody raved over her. I am always struggling to catch up with last year's news.

I can remember writing that as a journalist I am expected by members of the public to have access to tickets for every sporting event under the sun. I should have added that I am also expected to be a walking enyclopaedia of sporting knowledge, able to identify every athlete of whatever kind, rattle off who won what and when, and settle instantly arguments on arcane points such as which horse came third in the 1987 Derby and who was cox of the Oxford boat in 1922. To expect this of any man is as unreasonable as to expect every judge to have heard of the Beatles.

Old master in the loft

One of the most remarkable men I have known died not long ago. He was wrapped up in sport in one way or another all his life. His name is irrelevant. Few readers of this newspaper will have come across him, but in spite of – I would prefer to say because of – that fact, he deserves a word or two here.

I first knew him as a schoolmaster. He never taught me regularly and my clearest recollection of that time, during the last war, is of being hauled up in front of him for playing truant, for which he let me off with a caution.

The years passed. I left school, and eventually home, and lost contact with him. When by chance I began to meet him again he had retired from schoolmastering and turned to part-time sports journalism which suited his restless nature. He had no formal training for the work, but he knew and loved sport in a score of its manifestations, and made a small, enjoyable living.

He won university Blues, at athletics, cricket, football, swimming and water polo, one of them at Cambridge. He played cricket for a Scottish county, some reserve games for a first division football club, ran the marathon and sprinted. Once, in his sixties, he turned out for a midweek rugby team when they were short. Every year if possible he came from the far north to Lord's for a Test match. To the end of his days he was a rugby coach to small boys, and a swimmer.

He wrote mostly about rugby and cricket, in a sober, factual style in which could be heard echoes of the classroom. When I returned home on holiday he would meet me for coffee in the art gallery, bring me up to date on the local sporting intelligence, and, with gusto and humour, recount his latest journalistic exploits, mistakes and all.

The gusto and humour were needed. At the kind of grounds he frequented there were no press boxes, no programmes, often no shelter or telephones – a lack of amenities that would drive some pampered Fleet Street hacks to apoplexy. He had to dig for the simplest information and rely on an old friend, a 1914–18 veteran, to "run" his copy.

He used to call himself a Peter Pan, and it was a fair description of one so energetic and interested. His approach to life and sport was boyish, omnivorous, sociable, humble, without cynicism or rancour. Had it been otherwise, I doubt somehow whether he would have lived as long or done as much.

Shortly after his death, I visited his widow. She was at a loss to know what to do with his vast accumulation of sporting memorabilia strewn around the loft. We climbed up a ladder to look and she told me I could have anything I wanted.

The loft was big enough at one end to house a bed, in which, she said, he died one Saturday night. After a day spent reporting cricket, he had climbed up there to sleep, as was his frequent eccentric custom, and when he failed to come down next morning she went and found him.

He was eighty years old and had died among his Wisdens, Playfairs and Rothmans, his Carduses, Robertson-Glasgows, Arlotts and Swantons, his magazines, photographs, notebooks, press cuttings and programmes, going back years and years. Was it not a fitting end?

3
Where do Harlequins Come From?

Christmas in Llanelli

There can be much more to going to a rugby match than going to a rugby match. In the right circumstances, not seeing it can provide an experience to remember long after you would have forgotten the match itself.

One Christmas I was sent to Stradey Park to report Llanelli's game with Bath. I was looking forward to it because although I had seen the Llanelli team play, I had never seen their ancestral home. I have still not seen it.

The morning papers gave an evening kick-off, and so I travelled in the afternoon, intending to stay the night – if you follow my meaning. The little train from Swansea carried me up-country to Llanelli, and when I stepped out in the dusk I found the town like a sort of landlocked Marie Celeste – everywhere closed, the streets empty, not so much as a cat to be seen, and rain starting to fall.

My first task was to find a bed for the night, but I found only bolts and bars and unlit windows. Compassless, I walked in circles. When time pressed, I decided to go to the match first and look for a hotel later. But I had no idea where Stradey was, and there was nobody to ask because (I assumed) the entire population were either indoors being festive or already in their seats awaiting the kick-off.

It was getting colder by the minute, and the rain by now was pelting down. I sheltered in a shop doorway to review the situation, and as I stood there wet and shivering a policeman joined me. We fell into conversation, as men will when they meet unexpectedly on a desert island, and after agreeing with him that it was no night to be out, I mentioned the match.

"Oh, I've just come from Stradey," he said. "Wasn't much of a game. You didn't miss anything, believe me."

"But I understood it was in the evening."

"No, no. It kicked off at three, I think."

The referee, then, must have been blowing his whistle to end the match at about the time my train was arriving in Llanelli.

"Who won?" I asked, lugubriously.

"Sorry, I couldn't tell you that. I was on duty – had to leave before the end, see. But I think the Scarlets were leading."

I felt vaguely relieved. I did not need a hotel now because I could return to London that night, but I did need something to eat, and at last I found a pub, bought ham sandwiches and an orange juice, and, from my corner, overheard some of the customers discussing the match. They corroborated the policeman's opinion that it had been poor stuff.

"Fortunes of war, old chap," the office said when I reached them on the phone after half an hour of trying, and they wished me a happy new year. But I was sorry not to have seen Stradey Park, for I "collect" rugby grounds, no matter whose they are, Llanelli's or the London Fire Brigade's.

Twickenham party

Middlesex sevens day at Twickenham is beloved by hundreds of people who never go near a rugby match at any other time in the season. They go to the sevens as they would to a garden party, to see and be seen, as far as that is practicable in a crowd of 50,000-plus, although from time to time they may deign to glance at the pitch in the hope of seeing something thrilling – a streaker, perhaps, or a boy friend scoring a try, or both.

A peculiar clan, these folk, as peculiar as those who only go to internationals, club matches being beneath their notice. They go to internationals to see and be seen, and also to have lunch in the Twickenham car park because they have been told it is the Done Thing. I have never lunched in a car park. I am sure it would spoil my appetite to be surrounded by Alfa Romeos and Ford Cortinas, and I like smoked salmon too much to run that risk.

I know it is a free country, but I sometimes think, with my customary lack of humour in such matters, that people who know nothing about rugby should somehow be debarred from these occasions. They may be depriving genuine enthusiasts of tickets. But that is not my theme here. My theme – unthinkable in the 1960s and much of the 1970s – is that I have gone off the Middlesex sevens.

I used to look forward to them every year, but not now. They have become too brassy. The sight and sound of 50,000 people having a good time bring out the misanthrope in me, and the messages boomed over the public address system between games – about wives accidentally locked in the woodshed, or husbands suddenly called away on business to Alaska – no longer seem funny.

Then there is that long and awkward gap before the final,

now filled by displays, usually military, accompanied by relentless commentary over the loudspeaker. The horrible effect is of a television pundit's voice magnified a thousandfold. While waiting for the final I have sought refuge from the noise in the streets round Twickenham, but it is so deafening it pursues you. The standard of the sevens is not what it was, either. When I went every year I could see masters of the game such as Ken Scotland, Iain Laughland, Tremayne Rodd, Gerald Davies, Billy Hullin, John Dawes, Keith Fielding, Tony Bucknall and Roger Shackleton. Where are their peers now? Their successors look stereotyped, just as they do in fifteen-a-side.

The Border sevens, particularly Melrose, with its family-outing atmosphere, are far more enjoyable than the Middlesex: more relaxed, less strident, probably more skilful, at least these days.

Seven's a crowd

One of my professional ambitions is to report some sports event where there are no spectators – not even the traditional man, boy and barking dog – and no other journalists. I do not think it would be in the least dull, and in any case it would provide me with a "scoop" of sorts that I could brag about in barren moments.

The nearest I have come to it was a rugby match between the London Fire Brigade and the United States Navy at Hayes, Kent, two weeks before Christmas in 1967. Almost the entire rugby programme that day had been cancelled because of snow, and when I suggested covering this match *The Times*, instantly recognizing an important occasion, agreed.

There were, as far as I could see which, in the wintry light, was not very far, seven spectators, including the Navy captain (injured), their coach, and your correspondent. The Americans arrived thirty-five minutes late and had to borrow a fireman to make up their number. Both teams consisted of fourteen players, one of whom wore cricket boots. There were no touch judges. By mutual consent the match was restricted to twenty minutes each way. The Fire Brigade won 32-0. It was coarse rugby in all its glory.

And there was a sequel. Late one night someone from the US Navy, a little the worse for drink, rang the office from somewhere in Mayfair to tell me that I had got one of my facts wrong, although he did not make it clear which fact.

That match, with its seven spectators (six, if you care to split hairs and exclude the national press), has remained in my memory while countless others, attended by hysterically cheering multitudes, have gone for ever. Disliking people in the mass, and not being a club treasurer, I am uninterested in attendances, "gates", crowds.

But public opinion is different. Where football particularly is concerned, I hear more and more people wanting to know how many were at this match or that, and whether it was a record crowd or not, as though the information could somehow add to their knowledge of or pleasure in the game itself.

"What was the gate, mate?"

"The paper says 125,316."

"That all? Chickenfeed. I'm not going there again. No atmosphere."

Similar talk can be overheard among teenage "fans" going home in the train from a match late on a Saturday after-noon. First they describe the "aggro" they have enjoyed at the expense of the other team's "fans". Then they argue about the size of the crowd, those in favour of 500,000 pouring scorn on the pessimists who guess 250,000. Finally, but by no means always, and with the air almost of an irrelevant afterthought, they might discuss the game.

I exaggerate, of course, but it is difficult not to, because at the time I am usually returning from a rugby match that was watched by two or three hundred, if as many. Dropping the average club rugby crowd into a first division football crowd would be like adding a glass of water to the Atlantic. It is just as well I am not subject to inferiority complexes about numbers. If I were, all those digits and noughts flying around the carriage would be enough to make me curl up under the seat. But I never did have a head for figures.

Life without "boot money"

My rugby-playing career lasted about seven years. My greatest disappointment in that time was not my failure to play for the first fifteen, which I could well understand, but the fact that I never found anything in my boots.

How often have I gone into the dressing-room before some important match for the third or fourth team, peered inside my boots, and found them devoid even of an Irish sixpence. How often, too, have I tottered from the field at the end of the match, lifted down my jacket from its peg, put my hand in the inner pocket, and come out with no more than an old bus ticket.

And a little later when, showered and refreshed, I was enjoying my hard-earned cup of tea, did a sportswear manufacturer disguised as a spectator, a club official or a reporter ever sidle up and make me an offer? Not a bit of it. I endured seven years of such neglect; seven years of mud and blood; seven years of waiting with a cup of tea in my hand; seven wasted years.

The sportswear manufacturers did not know what they were missing. I would have worn anything they wanted me to wear, short of a kilt. Boots would have been only the start (they could have had hollow soles for the cheques). What about the latest fashion in headbands? Of course. Or socks? Pleasure's mine. A jersey with a plunging neckline? Inimitably me, I'm sure. A new brand of jock-strap? I'd try anything once.

Price is the only point I might have haggled over. I am not talking about money: only the dullest dog wants that alone as his reward. If they had wanted to throw in some money as a kind of makeweight I would have been grateful. But the other possibilities would have interested me more.

These sportswear people, it seems to me, lack imagination. They think that money, first and foremost, is what the poor rugby player is hoping to find in his boot. They are wrong. Not all players, not even all prop forwards, are as unimaginative as the manufacturers. A select few, of whom I was one, regard the boot in the same way as they used to regard their Christmas stocking. I know I would have felt hurt and deprived if as a small boy I had opened my stocking and found, instead of toys and books and games and sweets, a bunch of soiled banknotes.

I grew up with this nonconformist attitude almost untarnished. When I was a player money would never have appealed to my romantic instincts. I would prefer to have looked inside my boot and found a charming letter from the manufacturers inviting me to a meeting to discuss a suitable reward.

There, over coffee and biscuits (for I am as near teetotal as does not matter), I could have suggested, perhaps, an island of my own in some warm ocean where I could relax during the close season; or a private bowling green or snooker hall, with swimming pool attached, where I could indulge my other pastimes; or, if these were out of the question, the complete works of a dozen of my favourite writers, from Turgenev to Henry Miller, and/or records of a hundred pieces of music I like, from *Calon Lan* (to remind me of Cardiff Arms Park) to Bruckner's seventh symphony. These are only examples. Depending on mood, I might have asked for something quite different, such as a grand piano or a country bungalow within walking distance of the sea. But they illustrate what I mean about wanting what money can buy rather than the money itself: the ends rather than the means. It would be far more amusing and civilized to do business on those terms than to accept, almost at second hand, that bunch of soiled banknotes, like any old common-or-garden mercenary.

Oh Dear Park

On a fine Saturday afternoon I took my wife to her first rugby match. I chose London Welsh versus Harlequins at Old Deer Park. Why, you might ask, did I take her to a club match and not an international? The answer is that I wanted her to sample the game at its most typical, and internationals are no more typical of rugby than Test matches are of cricket or salmon steaks of a proletarian diet.

Besides, international status does not in the least guarantee quality and excitement. The dullest match I ever saw, at any level, was England against South Africa at Twickenham in 1961. South Africa won 5—0 and if Hopwood had not scored a good try, there would have been eighty minutes worth forgetting instead of seventy-nine.

My wife is not sport-minded. She played the obligatory

netball at school, she is tolerant of cricket, having been brought up in Surrey at the time of May, Laker, Lock and the Bedsers, and for my sake she occasionally sits through *Rugby Special* on television or remarks that she might try her hand on the bowling green one day. Otherwise, games leave her cold.

When we agreed to go to Old Deer Park she probably thought that because I write about rugby for a living I must know all about it and could enlighten her on any given point. If such was her assumption, it was unwarranted. I secretly hoped she would not expose the many gaps in my knowledge by asking abstruse questions. These gaps can be concealed easily enough by a cunning writer. It is a different matter altogether to be questioned to your face, innocently and without warning.

The start was not auspicious. As we drove past the deer in Richmond Park on our way to the ground she asked me, out of the blue, why a rugby ball is the shape it is. Has it always been like that or did it so develop? I had to confess I did not know. Perhaps because of this revelation the rest of the journey was completed in silence.

Old Deer Park looked its best: sunlit, deep green, busy with hockey and rugby players, chirpy with spectators, the Kew pagoda exotic above the trees – a fresco of early spring to open out the spirit. There, I thought, is a sight to disabuse anybody of the notion that rugby is all mud and scrums and violence. We went into the pavilion for a cup of tea and then walked across the field to take our seats in the stand.

Out trotted the teams and the match began. "Who's that man in yellow?" my wife asked. "The referee," I replied, proud to be so well informed. Rees scored a try for the Welsh and George converted. The conversion ritual led my wife to say that she had not realized that the ball could be stood up "like an egg."

I was glad that the first try she had seen was an excellent concerted effort. Almost at once Wall scored a soft try for Harlequins and, from a spot just in front of us, Dudman converted with a kick that enabled us to appreciate his judgment and the ball's curve inside the far post.

"Where do the Harlequins come from?" my wife asked. "Twickenham," I told her, quick as a bullet, regretting at the same time that, with their picturesque name, they did not come from somewhere less prosaic: Wyoming or Timbuktu would have sounded better.

After the two tries the standard of play fell. Stoppages for injuries and penalties multiplied. "Is that the doctor?" my wife asked when a track-suited figure clutching a bucket scuttled on to the pitch. "No", I said, "it's only the man with a sponge that heals everything except broken limbs and death."

She also wanted to know why the players persisted in kicking the ball over the stand. I tried to explain that the kicking was done to avert danger or gain ground and that the stand, as such, had no more to do with it than the Great Wall of China.

I made no attempt to elucidate the principal laws, or to explain everything that happened. I left it to her to ask. In the event I got off lightly because she asked only one question that could be called technical. She wondered why they always passed the ball backwards when they were supposed to be going forward. She thought it cockeyed. She also wished there was a goalkeeper. Someone like that, she said, gave a focal point to a game. The variety of scoring in rugby was confusing to her.

Harlequins won 9—6. Dudman landed the winning penalty goal. George and Slater each hit a post with penalty shots for the Welsh. Frustration wore a scarlet jersey. The crowd took umbrage at some of the referee's decisions. My wife perceived that referees have "a terrible job."

But on the whole the crowd were rather quiet, which meant that she experienced little of the hoped-for Welsh atmosphere. Some years ago, I told her, when the Welsh supplied seven

British Lions, things would have been different. That team would have annihilated Harlequins, to a deafening tumult. Even my wife could see it was a nondescript match. It had a beginning and an end but no middle. Unprompted, she said there was so much whistle that nothing was allowed to happen, and thereby showed she has the makings of a rugby critic.

Turkey Street memories

I reported the Hospitals Cup for many years. It is an enjoyable competition and institution if, as I do, you have no high-falutin' notions about rugby and consider one match to be much like another.

Apart from anything else, it has been one of my ways of learning the topography of London. If I had never become embroiled in the Cup, I might still not know where such delightful spots on the earth's surface as Turkey Street, Dog Kennel Hill and Copse Hill are. As Arthur Machen wrote in *The London Adventure*: "We all know about Piccadilly and Oxford Street, London Bridge and the Strand. Olympia has made us familiar with a little island in otherwise unknown Hammersmith: the Boat Race illuminates Putney, and the most inexperienced have ventured into High Street, Kensington. But where will you be if I ask you about Clapton, about the inner parts of Barnsbury, about the delights of Edmonton, about that region which was once called Spa Fields? Nay: how many people know their Camden Town in any thorough and intelligent manner?"

Turkey Street, in case you do not know, is in Enfield. It

is where the Royal Free have their ground and there are moments when you wish they had it in a more accessible location. Another intrepid Hospitals Cup scribe once went in good faith to Guy's ground at Honor Oak Park, in Brockley, and found that the match had been transferred at a late hour to Turkey Street. So he turned round and drove back across London, arriving at Turkey Street in time for the final whistle. His report next morning was as comprehensive as ever.

I mentioned Dog Kennel Hill, where King's play, not because you would wish to spend a holiday in east Dulwich in preference to the Tyrol, but because of its delightful name. Copse Hill, in Wimbledon, is delightful in its own right. St George's play there, in the green and sloping grounds of Atkinson Morley's Hospital, and when a player is injured it has been known for somebody to slip into the adjacent operating theatre to ask for water and bandages.

You have to learn the hard way that the only certainty about the Hospitals Cup is its uncertainty, almost its secrecy, on and off the field. It is advisable, before setting out, to check that the match is really and truly on and that it is being played where you are going, not on the other side of the metropolis. And when you get there you will be lucky if all the players are wearing numbers and even luckier if they are wearing the right ones, not to mention the right colours.

People like full backs and scrum halves are identified easily enough, numbers or no numbers. They have their set tasks in set places and you can keep track of them. It is the forwards who present problems, being in a sense of no fixed abode on the pitch, often in a heap, and tending mostly to look alike in length and breadth. If one wears a headband and another has red hair, how grateful you can be for such small mercies.

I am not complaining. These are the hazards of the Hospitals Cup and I accept them as a sailor accepts the risk of seasickness. Whether the Cup has always been like that, I cannot say; it was, after all, begun in 1875, when my grandfather was a stripling. But I would not be surprised if it has.

Nor would I be surprised if fun and farce and practical jokery have always been just below the surface, ready for full expression on the day of the final. I remember one hospital hiring a baby elephant from Whipsnade, bringing it in a van to Richmond, and parking it at the Kew end of the pitch.

In recent years we have seen much less of this theatre of the absurd, as if dowdy convention was overtaking medical students and nurses. But there is no guarantee that its doors will not fly open again or that, as once happened, the correspondent of *The Times* will not be burnt in effigy again for being too critical of supporters' horseplay.

Matches and monarchs

Match of the Day, Goal of the Week, Manager of the Month, Team of the Season, Player of the Year – where will it all end? It must end somewhere, since time must have a stop, and I would suggest, after careful consideration of twenty-four hours as a sensible limit, that we play the game on its own terms and accept twelve months and not a minute over.

It is silly to talk about the match of the century, for the simple, merciful reason that few of us live to be one hundred, and preposterous to talk about the greatest match of all time, whatever all time might mean. A year it is, then, and no more nonsense about comparing players and matches generations apart.

These labels are a publicity stunt – a fact not obvious, it seems, to many otherwise intelligent people. I am not qualified to discuss football, but in rugby I know that matches, teams and players all come more or less alike to me in the end.

Andy Hancock, with the ball, is challenged by David Whyte during the England-Scotland match at Twickenham in 1965, when Hancock scored his famous last-minute try to earn England a 3–3 draw. (Photograph: Sport & General)

Whether and how I remember them may well depend less on their quality than on the circumstances in which I see them.

This is emphatically true of matches. I may have witnessed a match of the day here or a match of the century there without realizing it. While thousands tried, far into the night, to articulate the immortal glory of events on the field, I retired to bed early with a good book. It is remiss of me, but as I say, it usually takes something other than the rugby to fix a match in my mind.

The England-Scotland match of 1965 lives on for me because it was the first time I entered the press box at Twickenham. That is the first reason. The second is that I sat between two grizzled and distinguished correspondents, one of whom asked if I had ever played. In an orgy of wishful thinking I answered: "Yes. Scotland, Barbarians and British Lions."

The third reason is that when the Queen, a tiny figure in blue, and doubtless radiant, appeared in the stand opposite, one of these correspondents leant across to the other in breathless excitement, exclaiming: 'It's the Monarch, Harold, the Monarch". The fourth reason – and I mean fourth in my order of importance – is that Andy Hancock scored his famous try.

Now you get it. Now you understand my view. "It's the Monarch, Harold, the Monarch".

Dropping some goals

Someone remarked to me recently that too little use is made of the dropped goal in rugby. Often, he said, you will see a team create the perfect situation for a dropped goal – a scrummage in front of the posts – and then ignore it. Instead of grasping the three points lying under their noses, they go for the try, irrespective of whether they need the extra points or not, and rue doing so when, for instance, the outside centre bungles his pass to the wing with the goalline a yard away.

The question has other aspects, of course. One team may use the threat of a dropped goal as a stratagem to catch the other's defence off guard. The stand-off half, having pointedly gone deep behind his scrum half as though preparing to drop a goal, is equally pointedly left out of the totally different manoeuvre that follows, and the crowd gaze in vain at the sky between the posts. It may also happen that the ball comes back too sluggishly for a dropped goal to be feasible, or even that nobody thinks of dropping a goal, however obvious it seems from the ropes.

A further point that occurs to me is that dropped goals are arguably less well remembered than tries and may therefore seem less common than they really are. A dropped goal is the work of an instant, like one of Bertie Wooster's inspirations. Tom, Dick or Harry swings a leg, over soars the ball, the crowd applaud – and that, apparently, is that.

A try, on the other hand, may take two or three minutes to score and be a thing of beauty, if not a joy forever. The ball may travel the entire length of the pitch, pass through a dozen pairs of hands, and finish up in the mud beside the corner flag, grounded there by Duckham, Gerald Davies, or some other popular hero on the wing. No wonder, then, that we remember tries: Obolensky's, Wilson Shaw's, Cliff Morgan's, Jackson's, Hancock's, Sharp's, and so forth. To rugby followers the scorers' names are the shorthand for a single, unmistakable time, place and occasion, yesterday, the day before, or long ago.

The much abused penalty goal takes time, too, especially if a kicker as methodical and phlegmatic as Hiller is attempting it. It can build up its own tension, tying a knot inside the spectator, making him want to look the other way. Its ritual can be dramatic, with a breathless audience hanging on the denouement. It is therefore food for the memory, like the try. Remember Grimsdell's penalty for London Counties against the South Africans in 1951. Remember Irvine's last-minute penalty for Scotland against England in 1974. They were match-winning kicks. Remember Geffin, Villepreux, Kiernan, Hosen, Barry John and Doble. Remember the long line of men who have been known (not always affectionately) as "The Boot".

When it comes to recalling dropped goals, they, as I said, seem at first to be more elusive. But persevere, and Kininmonth's improbable one for Scotland against Wales in

1951 may come back to you. He was near the touchline and hemmed in. He dropped at goal, presumably more in hope than expectation, and the ball went over. Scotland won 19—0, after widespread predictions of the opposite result. The story goes that the next time Kininmonth tried to drop a goal – in a club match at Richmond – the ball landed nearer the corner flag than the posts.

That match of Kininmonth's dropped goal was one of only two sporting events on which I have gambled. In each case I won a shilling and in each my faith was considerable to the point of foolhardiness. The other was the FA Cup final of 1953, the year of Matthews. Blackpool were 1–3 down to Bolton Wanderers when, beside a radio in Berlin, I put my piece of silver on Blackpool to win.

But back to dropped goals. I have been told that Herbert Waddell rarely played for Scotland without dropping a goal. I remember Dorward, the Scotland scrum half, kicking one similar to Kininmonth's, also against Wales, in 1957. I remember Uzzell's dropped goal for Newport against the All Blacks in 1963. I remember Hawthorne kicking three for Australia against England in 1967: Hawthorne, who, with Catchpole, made half back play look so easy and natural and unhurried.

So is the dropped goal too little used? Such things cannot be computed. But whatever the truth, the dropped goal is usually the result of initiative and quick thinking, of inspired reflex action, which is more than can be said of the machine-made penalty. It is often exciting to see, particularly when you are not expecting it, as you often do not. It can buck up a team and a game. It used to be worth four points. It is still worth four.

Multi-phase possession

Chris Rea, a former Scotland and British Lions centre three-quarter, has described second-phase possession in rugby as "that evil little phrase" and said that whoever thought it up should be condemned for eternity to the Gloucester wing. Such phrases make an interesting study. Nobody is sure where they originate, but once in circulation they are on everybody's lips and pen-nibs.

Most of them have sprung up during the past ten or fifteen years. *Second-phase possession* is, I think, the oldest and commonest. It is the type of possession to which all teams aspire because it is supposed to produce more tries than any other. In their attempts to make assurance doubly sure, they even go as far as a third or fourth phase. The forwards barely have time to disentangle themselves from one ruck before they have to plunge into another, all in the name of theory. The theory is plausible enough, but there seems little point in insisting on it unless you perfect the practice first, which rarely happens. This insistence is one of the reasons why, to the chagrin of the idealists, penalty goals rather than tries continue to decide most matches.

Front five is a more recent phrase but scarcely less popular. Its precursor was *the front row*. At one time it was generally believed that matches were won and lost in the front row. Those who take binoculars to Twickenham as others take opera-glasses to Covent Garden glued them to props and hookers as a matter of course and read all kinds of recondite meanings into the activities of those workers at the scrum face, as Norman Mair once called them. If one prop heaved his opponent into the air it was considered an event of far-reaching significance. There was – still is – much debate about loose-heads and tight-heads, even among people who, like me, can never remember which is which.

However, the emphasis has now shifted from the front row to the front five. If the front five are all right, everything else, the experts say, falls into place. Mention the front five and your reputation as a technically knowledgeable rugby man is secure, just as, if you chatter about C sharps and semi-quavers, you can be mistaken for somebody with a profound understanding of music. There is no vogue yet for the back three. But be patient. Sooner or later the decisive influence they exert will be recognized with a shout of "Eureka!" and the front five will be forced to take a back seat.

Then there is the case of the neglected *lineout jumpers*. Like many obvious things in life, they have been around a long time but apparently unnoticed. Now, in belated remorse, we are falling over one another to appreciate what they do. We have allotted them numbers, with specific responsibilities, and say that Black is second to none as a jumper at two and White out of this world at four, and that if Grey plays to form at seven, England will be in easy street.

Or what about *crash-ball*? There is a phrase to conjure with. Better (or rather, worse) is *crash-scissors-ball*. My eyes crossed when I first read that. It was supposed to convey something about rugby to me. Instead, being obtuse, I saw a vision of cars piling up in fog on the motor-way ludicrously superimposed on another vision of innumerable pairs of scissors snipping the laces of innumerable rugby balls.

Eventually I worked out what crash-scissors-ball meant – at least I think I did. But for much longer than I should have been, I was as mystified by the description as the players doubtless were by the move. From *good-ball*, another piece of jargon but intelligible, to crash-scissors-ball is a long way.

The central truth about the modern scientific approach to rugby, of which these phrases are the vocabulary, is that it has done nothing for the game as a spectacle. Famous players of the past readily concede it is better organized now, but you rarely, if ever, hear them say it is better to watch. You can, in fact, organise your fifteen men until you and they are dizzy, but in the end it all comes back to the individual. Blend individual genius with a high ratio of collective skill, and organization justifies itself brilliantly. Witness Wales for the past decade, the Lions in New Zealand in 1971, London Welsh in the Dawes era. But no amount of organization, down to the umpteenth phase of possession and the last crash-ball (with or without scissors), can leave mediocrity anything but mediocre.

The tartan strollers

Many years ago I watched the Middlesex sevens for the first time. The winners were London Scottish, who beat Stewart's College FP, of Edinburgh, 20–6 in the final. Scottish had won the previous year, too, and went on to win in 1962, 1963 and 1965. They should have won in 1964 but made uncharacteristic tactical and defensive mistakes against Loughborough College in the final and lost 18–16 in the last minute.

The Scottish seven were a great team, complete and balanced. They were acknowledged as great then and their reputation has not diminished in the slightest as subsequent Twickenham winners have come and gone. If anything, it has increased, to the point of being legendary. Every year, before Scottish emerge from the tunnel, the announcer, Peter Yarranton, refers to their past glories, as if hoping that they might somehow bear him out by playing like their predecessors. It could never be. Since 1965 those in the crowd

Tremayne Rodd scores for London Scottish against Blackheath in the 1965 Middlesex sevens. (Photograph: Sport & General).

who never saw Scottish in their meridian have had to take the stories of their prowess and artistry on trust.

Scottish appeared in six consecutive Twickenham finals, a record. They also equalled the record of four consecutive wins established by Harlequins between 1926, the first year of the tournament, and 1929. Iain Laughland, in the opinion of some the greatest sevens three-quarter ever seen at Twickenham, and Jim Shackleton played in all six finals, surpassing the record of W. W. Wakefield, who played for Harlequins in 1926-29.

Scottish spread the word beyond Twickenham. In 1962, for instance, they won the Melrose, Sussex and Paris University sevens, and in 1965 they won at Melrose, Hawick and North Kent. Melrose, where the short game originated in 1883, has been called the blue riband of sevens tournaments, and you have to be no less good to win at Hawick. But it was at Twickenham that Scottish first made their name.

Norman Mair has said that Scottish did for sevens what the Hungarians did for football. Mike Williams, who played against Scottish at Twickenham, wrote in his book *Rugby Sevens*: "Their performance was a real revolution, a revelation of what was possible with a little thought, a little practice and a few gifted players." Teams such as Hawick have excelled them in the number of tournaments won but not in individual and collective flair.

They evolved and perfected the possession game. Possession and support were their watchwords. Other teams ran hither and thither, shedding energy in all directions, relying on fitness, speed and strength rather than subtlety. Scottish, equally fit, fast and strong but twice as subtle, reduced the tempo, sometimes to a walk, thereby conserving their own energy – an important consideration in sevens – and making their opponents uneasy.

Once they had the ball they rarely lost it, and made sure there was always support within five yards of the ball-carrier, regardless of the tactical situation. While waiting for a gap to appear in the opposition defence, they amused themselves – and the crowd – by tracing intricate patterns around the pitch, until the ball resembled a toy on the end of an infinitely stretchable piece of elastic. The gap duly appeared and through it for a try went Tremayne Rodd, Ronnie Thomson, or whoever happened to be handy.

It sounds easy; it looked easy; but only Scottish were talented enough to play it that way. Laughland said that Scottish practised several nights a week. "We often did nothing but practise passing for threequarters of an hour. But that's the secret of it." Little wonder they dropped so few passes or that, after a season or two, other teams went out to play them with an inferiority complex.

Laughland's first appearance in a Scottish seven was in 1957, when they lost to St Bartholomew's Hospital in the

Middlesex preliminaries at Beckenham. His last was ten years later, when they lost to Harlequins in the sixth round. In his prime he was compared to Harry Lind, who played for two winning sevens at Twickenham – the Barbarians in 1934 and the London Scottish in 1937. He said that he was indebted for much of his sevens knowledge to Ken Scotland, who was also compared to Lind and who played in the successful Scottish seven in 1960 and 1961.

Although Laughland was not always captain of the seven, he was unquestionably their tactical general. And he was fortunate in his lieutenants over the years: Thomson, Shackleton, Rodd and Stewart Wilson in the backs, Robin Marshall, Cameron Boyle, Rory Watherston and John Brash, among others, in the forwards. Rodd (scrum half), Laughland (stand-off) and Shackleton (centre) formed the most feared midfield triangle of their time and, with Thomson on the wing, an ideal sevens back division. Nobody could tell what Rodd would do next. Shackleton combined power, speed and grace. Thomson was probably as quick as Keith Fielding or Gerald Davies.

Marshall, who captained the Scottish seven in 1962 and 1963, said: "Laughland's startling changes of either pace or direction were well known, but he had much more than that: his strategic thinking and his work-rate in covering and in backing-up were not highly enough appreciated but were, in fact, very much in the manner of Mike Gibson. He was outstanding in an unusually gifted sevens backline. The balance won't be matched for a very long time."

In 1966, after six consecutive Twickenham finals, Scottish were beaten by Harlequins in the sixth round. It was the end of an era and I wrote: "The ideas were still there but not the pace of yore to carry them through. The magic had faded. But it is safe to say that the tournament has never been won by subtler or more vivid sevens than Scottish put into the field in their finest years."

Banish the lineout

Everybody in rugby agrees, tacitly or otherwise, that the lineout is a mess, and everybody, from the International Board to the equally important gentlemen in the Old Rottinghamians pack, has his own remedies for it. The only suggestion I have never seen, perhaps because it is so obvious, is that it should be scrapped altogether.

The lineout creates more problems than it solves. In the unlikely event of nobody being obstructed, lifted or offside, the possession that follows is usually about as much use to the long-suffering scrum half as a kick in the head, which he may receive anyway as a result of bad tapping or deflecting. As often as not, a ruck or maul forms as soon as the lineout ends, with no clear advantage to either side. After that may come the additional threat of a set scrummage. And so on, with one stoppage leading to another.

In place of the lineout, I suggest, with due diffidence, a football-style throw-in, though not, of course, towards the opposition goalline. It could be either straight across the field or towards your own goalline, and any distance you like. Think how much simpler the game would become, for players, referees and spectators, and how much more fluid. Unforeseen problems would crop up, no doubt, but they could not possibly be more numerous and frustrating than those of the lineout.

It is when players coalesce, as they do at scrummages and lineouts, that the trouble starts and offences multiply. There is, however, a compactness about scrummages which makes them superior to lineouts as a means of settling the argument over possession, and gives the ball a better chance of emerging quickly and controllably, with the minimum of interference.

There is no such compactness about lineouts. They straggle by nature, like ranks of raw guardsmen. Rain or shine, well timed jumping and two-handed catching are rare. So are successful peels. As for the short lineout, it is as much an admission of failure to solve the riddle of the lineout as it is a tactical move. All this means that the scrum halves are the most anxious men at the lineouts, and generally look it. Who can blame them? Even in international matches there is no guarantee that they will be saved by their forwards' skill from a hammering.

If the lineout went, the lineout signal would go with it. This would be a loss to those who see the funny side of the game. In a way the lineout signal is a symptom of what is wrong with the lineout. It is an attempt to shed light on a dark subject and hardly ever seems to work. You wonder, as you listen to the tense chorus of instruction that precedes the throw-in and watch the confusion that frequently succeeds it, whether these secret codes are worth inventing.

One instance is graven on my memory. In a county championship match at Wareham, Dorset, the word Aberdeen was sung out as a lineout signal. Naturally I was gratified to hear the name of my native city being used intelligently instead of to connote a quite fictitious stinginess. But I was less gratified when I saw the result of the signal. The ball flew back several yards over the scrum half's shoulder, and the opposing forwards, rushing through on him, nearly scored.

Nor does it make any apparent difference what kind of signals are used. Numbers are the most popular, but I have also heard girls' names echoing across wintry parks, and authors' names like Charles Dickens, and the names of celebrities like Mickey Mouse. I would have thought it easier to remember names than a string of digits but I must be wrong. Who am I to question the significance of 765 or 481, or even 932? The only thing I am sure of, as a humble onlooker, is that they rarely seem to add up, in terms of winning the ball.

When I played rugby, which was neither yesterday nor the

day before, and then only at a rather coarse level, we did not have lineout signals. We lived in the unscientific, uncoached, unmotivated age, when wing three-quarters, not hookers, threw the ball in. We hatched no plots for the lineouts. I doubt if we would have been able. We just shambled into position and hoped for the best.

The lineout now, whatever the status of the match, is no more satisfactory than it was then, despite all the legislative tinkering. I do not suppose for a moment that it will be abolished in my lifetime, if ever. It is something to be lived with, like income tax. But contemplating the possibility of rugby without lineouts is agreeable utopian fun, much as contemplating beating the All Blacks once was.

Fall of rugby man

A sending-off in rugby can have its comical side. The first I saw – and that by chance – was at Esher on a wet Saturday morning. The culprit was a second fifteen forward who looked, beside the referee, about eight feet tall; or, to put it from another angle, the referee, if he had not had to crane his neck to the sky, would have been gazing at the player's navel.

I remember that tableau from the 1960s. Happy days. Sendings-off were rare then, and before that even rarer. An old Surrey player who saw Cyril Brownlie, the All Blacks forward, sent off at Twickenham in 1925 told me that being sent off in that era was so unusual as to be almost, in his words, a hanging offence. Now sendings-off are the weekly norm. The typical game of controlled physical violence has become much less controlled and much more violent.

I have no idea why, although I suspect that the increase in competition and the correspondingly inflated importance of winning come into it somewhere. But I prefer to leave such analysis to those who have more faith than I have in generalization.

Let them, if they wish, blame the violence on television. The most violent of the very few programmes I bother to watch happens to be none other than *Rugby Special*, and weeks can go by without my watching even that. So you see I am ill qualified to speak about either violence or television let alone some hypothetical connection between the two.

As for remedies, I suggest the automatic and immediate award by the referee of six points against any team who have a player sent off. It would be more effective than sermons from club chairmen and the RFU, and possibly a greater deterrent than suspensions.

I began playing and watching rugby in the 1940s and twenty years passed before I saw anybody sent off. Maybe I was just lucky. Then I saw the Esher incident and, around the same time, a Cardiff, Wales and Lions prop sent off at Coventry – and he was thought to have been unjustly penalized, if changing-room feeling was any guide. Now we have a referee walking off in disgust, a match in which three players are dismissed, and who knows what to come – perhaps the entire crowd going home at half-time.

So is violence on television to blame? Or another pet scapegoat, like the government or the press? Or is it just old Adam, a wily scoundrel and much feared forward in his day? Perhaps only at schoolboy level now can we be fairly sure of not bumping into him, of not seeing somebody sent off and the game disfigured.

Kicks and arias

I see that someone has written to *The Spectator* complaining about too much undeserved applause at opera performances. I would like to lodge the same complaint about equally frivolous occasions – rugby matches.

Anybody not brought up on rugby will invariably tell you that two things put them off it: the number of scrums and, in a game supposedly based on handling, the amount of kicking. Nobody in his right mind applauds a scrum, to which the natural reaction is a groan, but kicking can be cheered and clapped by thousands, even when, as is usually the case, nothing comes of it. Hence my complaint.

Skilful, premeditated kicking that puts a team into an attacking position, or clears a dangerous one, deserves applause. Reflex-action kicking that merely gets rid of the ball, to save the player the trouble of doing anything positive, ought to be greeted with scornful silence.

How often in the open field you see the ball kicked when there are three or four men waiting, gasping, longing for it outside the kicker. Even if that particular kick happens to find a good touch, it ought still to be treated as wasteful and a betrayal of the code.

A lot of rugby consists of this type of kicking. It is no less prevalent now than it was years ago, before kicking direct into touch between the twenty-five-yard lines was barred. No wonder that followers of other games, from football to tenpin bowling, are surprised at so many wanting to play and watch rugby. It must seem a game that promises far more than it fulfils, when they see two teams kicking their way up and down the field and, apart from yet more scrums, and the odd player sent off, little or nothing happening in consequence.

"Ten times I sat up expectantly," Sir Thomas Beecham said after hearing a Bruckner symphony, "and ten times I recoiled." Many a rugby match has the same effect, and aimless kicking is the chief cause. If applause for it were cut out there might be less disappointment. The players might notice the deathly hush and start using their hands in preference to their feet. After all, that is how most tries are scored.

4
Scrabble, and Other Diversions

Libido-before-wicket

NEWS ITEM: John McEnroe blamed the media and their intrusions on the private lives of players for hastening Bjorn Borg's retirement from tennis.

A short while ago I wrote about my disappointment that I never received any "boot money" during my distinguished career as a third fifteen rugby player. I was also disappointed that the media never intruded on my private life, because I could have told them a thing or two.

I was a wild provincial boy then. I have settled down since and married, and gone to live among stockbrokers and rising young estate agents in the suburbs, and I now prefer a reading lamp to the bright lights. But in those days it was different. Only death, illness or prison would have kept me out of night clubs and clip joints at weekends.

Away matches were the best. The married players liked them because they could escape from their wives and "home improvements" for the day. The unmarried ones liked them because they sometimes tired of the local scene and wanted to explore the dives of another town (not knowing, yet, that one dive is much like another). Really, the match was little more than an excuse for a beano afterwards.

Well do I remember those coach journeys. We were quiet enough on the outward run; we might even have a team talk, during which I could be asked, if not relied on, to mark the blind side in the forthcoming game. But mostly we sat and watched the cows and telegraph poles, or dozed, or read the sports pages, or, in certain unregenerate cases, thought about the evening ahead.

The homeward journey, late that night or early the next morning, was noisy, smoky, beery, and – stretching a point – musical. Some sang, in wavering unison, about the mating habits of the sturgeon or the fact that you cannot go to heaven in an old Ford car. One or two reeled up and down the gangway, bantering incoherently. Others compared notes about what they claimed to have seen or done – particularly done – after the match.

Our cricket, too, had its extra-curricular activities, its cities of the plain beyond the hedgerows. I was enlisted as an umpire and many were the Saturdays when, at drawing of stumps, miles from home and safe from detection, we exchanged whites for glad rags and dispersed to the hot spots, with banalities like victory or defeat forgotten, and l-b-w standing, as someone ought to have observed, for libido-before-wicket.

If the media, in their perennial Mills & Boon innocence, had ever approached us about all these carryings-on, we would have regarded it, not as an intrusion on our private lives, but as a chance to instruct the less experienced in the ways of the world. We would have assured them that they had not heard the half of it. We would have made their eyes pop and their ears burn. To mention only the mentionable, we would have told them about club jaunts to London and Hamburg and Paris and Amsterdam; about scrummages and long legs; about clandestine assignations during Calcutta Cup weekend or the Lord's Test match; about banana juice flowing like champagne and floor shows Olympic in their scope. And some of it would have been true. The only people who might have retired as a result of these scandalous but far from unique disclosures were the media themselves – probably into a monastery.

Such pleasures seem insipid now, and the media would have no cause to intrude on my private life. The emperor fully clothed is not news. They would not want to know that I am just like them – that I walk the dog, cut the lawn, and enjoy the occasional day trip to Hastings.

Lord's and Abinger

The cricket field itself was a mass of daisies and buttercups and dandelions, tall grass and purple vetches and thistledown, and great clumps of dark red sorrel, except, of course, for the oblong patch in the centre – mown, rolled, watered – a smooth, shining emerald of green, the Pride of Fordenden, the Wicket.

I first read those words before I had set foot in England. But even in those far-off days I knew something of village cricket, or at least cricket of roughly comparable standard, because my first editor was a good player and one Saturday he inveigled me into umpiring, explaining that the Frank Chester of his club was unavailable.

I was seventeen and grasshopper green at the time, although by no means ignorant about cricket. It was a league match, played at Montrose or some such place, and the first decision I was called on to give – a catch behind the wicket – was wrong, or so the luckless batsman mentioned to me afterwards, with pained tolerance.

Subsequently I stood quite often. My correct decisions must have outnumbered the other kind. Once, I am proud to relate, I was barracked – on the North Inch at Perth – when the last two batsmen of "my" side were together, time was nearly up, and the home crowd considered I was walking too slowly to and from square leg between overs.

In the army, too, I umpired – a different sort of guard duty, you could say. The field was at Bielefeld, a German town better known among the uniformed classes for its military prison, and I, a full private, gave the company sergeant-major out, a decision for which he did not care. He said – that pained tolerance again – that he never got a touch. He was a majestic, likeable man, with an Eighth Army ribbon, who told me that before the war he worked as a wall-of-death rider in a circus.

I can also say that I have umpired in an English village match. An uncle of mine was playing at a hamlet called Old, deep in the heart of Northamptonshire, and, like the editor, he inveigled me into the white coat. It is not any particular decision I recall from that afternoon but the fact that one of the fieldsmen, with his Midlands accent, and I, with my Scottish accent, completely failed to make ourselves understood when we tried to while away the time at square leg in civilized conversation.

Otherwise my experience of village cricket has been limited to watching. I like to go to Lord's one Saturday and Abinger Hammer the next and tell myself, for paradox is the spice of life, that there is little difference between the two. It seems to me that it all depends on attitude and on the spectacles you happen to be wearing.

Much pseudo-lyrical rubbish has been written about village cricket. Cardus himself was never at his best on the subject; he was a writer, in Robertson-Glasgow's opinion, "made for the mountain top". For his words to take him up there, he needed Maclaren or Bradman, Blythe or Grimmett, not the local blacksmith heaving sixes while the vicar's wife prepared the tea.

But the passage with which I began is not rubbish. It comes from A. G. Macdonell's description of a village match in *England, Their England*, a chapter he was wise enough to end thus: "... and Donald got home to Royal Avenue at one o'clock in the morning, feeling that he had not learnt very much about the English from his experience of their national game".

Bestriding the crease

I hesitate to lay the dead hand of topicality on what I write but it is unavoidable if the name of Geoffrey Boycott is mentioned. Boycott has been topical for years and seems likely to go on being topical for many more. There was a time when he was too topical even for some Yorkshiremen, and he is certainly too topical for me, because I shall now drop him like a catch in the slips and tell you the story of another difficult cricketer.

This man is no longer topical because he is dead. A few cricketers – Grace and Trumper, for example – are in a sense always topical, in spite of being dead. This man is not of their company. When he died, his topicality died with him.

He was a club cricketer and a bad one. Some were convinced he was the worst club cricketer who ever lived, though they, too, had claims to the distinction. He owed his place in the team mainly to the fact that his father, grandfather and great-grandfather had been pillars of the club as president, captain and everything else you can think of, including scorer.

Assuredly he did not owe it to his batting. He was scarcely ever known to reach double figures, yet insisted on going in first wicket down – Bradman's spot, as he called it. Nor did he owe it to his bowling, although he liked to see himself as the local Sobers, with three styles at his finger-ends. Sometimes you hear of players who are worth their place for their fielding alone; he was not one of them.

But if his batting, bowling and fielding left room for improvement, his ability to be elected captain season after season was amazing – amazing, that is, if you ignored his father, grandfather and great-grand-father, which was not easy, as their gilt-framed photographs glowered from almost every wall in the pavilion.

At annual meetings he would gesture at these photographs as at pictures of the monarchy and urge the members to uphold the club's traditions, which were negligible as far as success on the field went, but historically stretched back to the Indian Mutiny. He was an eloquent speaker, particularly after dinner, and what with his oratory, force of character, marriage to the daughter of a man who played once for MCC, and those presences on the walls, his return to power became in time a foregone conclusion.

There were resistance movements. Pressure groups met clandestinely in each other's houses, but could not press hard enough. The vice-captain resigned when a campaign to have him elected captain failed – and his batting average was Bradmanesque compared with the captain's.

The committee were in the captain's pocket; the president was the captain's father-in-law; two plus two equals four. Even the press was powerless: the editor of the local paper had fagged for the president at school and could not break the habit.

Now when a country gets into such a mess, it takes a revolution to change things. That usually involves assassinating the dictator. A cricket club is different, and this dictator's innings ended in un-revolutionary circumstances. He was knocked down crossing the road outside Lord's and passed away in hospital. The un-Christian opinion was that if he had been more athletic in the field, he could have avoided the car. His ashes were scattered over the club's pitch and his photograph, showing him bestriding the crease like a Colossus, was hung alongside those of his father, grandfather and great-grandfather.

The man who succeeded him has been captain for several years now, and at annual meetings is prone to wave at those photographs and remind the members of the club's traditions. What will happen in the next revolution, nobody knows.

Never "another Bradman"

There have been several "new Bradmans" since the Don retired in 1948, but none survived the comparison. It is an old journalistic ruse. Pluck a great player from the past, imagine you see his likeness in the latest rising star, and go on from there. Nobody believes you – nobody of any sense, that is – but it is worth a try and makes an eye-catching headline.

To suggest that any batsman is the "new Bradman" is not only a tribute to Bradman. You can also hear, if you listen hard, a simultaneous cautionary voice saying, "Don't believe a word of it. There can never be another Bradman".

The writer, an old hand, is at once flattering and deflating the pretender to the throne. He knows that a few centuries by a promising youngster do not make him a "new Bradman". He knows that Bradman, like Grace, is a nonpareil whose renown is not diminished a jot by the fact that his run-scoring records may occasionally be beaten. It is Bradman the whole man, Bradman the public figure, Bradman the legend he is thinking of, and not solely the "little devil" at the crease.

I speak as someone who did not become aware of cricket, let alone Bradman, until the evening of Bradman's career but who is happy to accept the testimony of those who knew and studied him. I had the chance to see his last innings in Britain – at Aberdeen in September 1948 – but for some reason did not take it, although my school was given the afternoon off for the occasion. He scored 123 in eighty-nine minutes.

I do not know the "new George Best" – judging by the current state of football, as described by the experts, that particular throne is vacant – but sooner or later we will be invited to suspend disbelief and think we are watching a comparable player. As in the case of Bradman, we are likely to watch in vain.

With Bradman we at least have his statistical achievements, which are easily cited. With Best it is much more a matter of mysterious, almost supernatural ability. He is said to have had genius, and genius is not measurable in statistics.

But that does not deter fanciful journalists from discovering the "new Best" whenever they want – whenever, perhaps, they have nothing better to do. No doubt there have been a few; I do not keep a count. One I remember is Peter Marinello, who played for Arsenal some years ago. He came from Hibernian with the reputation of being the "new Best", and it proved to be the equivalent of a boulder tied to each ankle. He sank rapidly and without trace. It was not his fault.

The "new Pelé – another favourite – is even less conceivable than the "new Best". The "new Barry John"? Hardly. "New Piggott"? Doubtful. "New Borg"? Ditto. "New Muhammad Ali"? Never. "New David Bryant"? No. "New Thingmejig and Thingmebob"? You must be joking.

It is all amusing pub talk, and a waste of breath. Leave the old masters in peace. They are a glorious minority, sufficient unto themselves. Just as important, leave the new masters in peace – having first ascertained that they are masters and not ordinarily talented pupils.

Adventure with Figaro

Sequels in any form are rarely as good as the originals. Hollywood loves them but *Return of the Seven* was a poor thing compared with *The Magnificent Seven*. All the same, making the short journey from the sublime to the ridiculous, I want to give our dog Figaro, a Labrador-retriever cross, a second run in these columns.

He first appeared nearly five years ago and much has happened, to him and us, since then. At one extreme the vet advised us to consider having him put down; at the other the president of the English Bowling Association, standing in full regalia on the pavilion steps at Beach House Park, Worthing, offered to buy him. In both cases our answer was no.

Figaro had given the vet and his staff a frightening time when he needed a small operation. "That dog is not just another soft Labrador but a risk," the vet said feelingly, and told us of an owner who, in similar circumstances, had the tip of his nose bitten off. We thought the matter over for a day or two; consulted a local dog trainer, a Scottish lady with a large picture of Wagner on her living-room wall; and Figaro lived.

With the EBA president we did not reach the point of discussing a price. Figaro would have been as happy on the fells of Cumbria, Mr President's home, as he is on the commons of Surrey – perhaps happier. But again, sentiment won.

Figaro is quite a travelled dog. Among his shorter excursions is one to Abinger Hammer, where we go some summer Saturdays to watch cricket. We take him in the car, which has been christened by me The Carriage of Figaro, have a cream tea and then climb a steeply sloping field for what amounts to a bird's eye view of the play.

Late one afternoon last year we were watching the wickets falling when fifteen or twenty cattle appeared at the far end of the field, wandered along the wire fence dividing it from the cricket ground, then turned and advanced on us up the hill. At first we thought that if we stayed where we were they would come so far and stop. But they were inquisitive beasts and plodded on in our direction.

Fearing what Figaro might do in this delicate situation – I had visions of a stampede and the farmer brandishing a shotgun – we sidled down towards the fence, followed by the cattle, and crawled out before they could surround us. In the meantime the cricket had stopped and the players and spectators were watching our performance, sensing the possibility of something more exciting than an l-b-w decision. I am afraid I cannot remember the result of their match.

Too much sport?

I can never make up my mind whether there is too much sport in this world or too little. The received opinion is that there is too much, but since that opinion is received from people who would have us spending all our time doing something "serious" and "responsible" like wallpapering or double glazing, instead of storing up health in the fresh air, it can be set aside *sine die.*

For the sake of a dash of fun – and profound conclusions have been reached in pursuit of fun – let us suppose there is too little sport and ponder how to correct the imbalance. Let us open our daily newspapers and wax indignant because only four pages, and those four at the back, mark you, are devoted to sport. There should be twelve at least, and those twelve near the front. Why, in an ideal world the front page itself would contain nothing but sports news, with general elections, national strikes and other trivia relegated to the back.

It may be that there are not enough sports to suit all tastes. In that case we had better invent some. Man cannot live by football alone, although millions try.

Inventing sports is quite easy. A year or two ago I suggested that walking the dog is a kind of sport, or at any rate pastime, which amounts to the same thing. I did not have to invent it; it was there already, as old as Noah, I imagine, and as popular a pastime as you will find in England – on a par with golf but without the frustration.

From dogs to frogs is a short hop, and I can remember a report of the world frog jumping championship, held somewhere abroad, appearing in *The Times.* It did not survive beyond the first edition, but that is beside the point. The point is that someone had been curious enough to find out if the competitive, or sporting, instinct is highly developed in frogs, and whether, perhaps, they might benefit from training and motivation.

I have seen a monkey being taken for a walk in the streets of London, which suggests, by extension of ideas, that monkeys, too, could be coaxed into racing in an organized way, maybe from tree to tree. The Tarzan Cup? Yet it would be wrong to rely on animals, even on those thought to be our close relatives, to satisfy our sporting instincts. It is too voyeuristic. Taking part is of the essence.

In Scotland they toss the caber. That indicates a rosy future for tossing the goalpost. There is a new sport for you – at least I think it is new. It would not be beautiful, but as a trial of strength it could scarcely be bettered.

Skateboarding has gone out of fashion but could be brought back and adapted to some ingenious new discipline. Underwater wrestling would go down well, and so might croquet on ice. Snakes and ladders in which people take the place of the counters on a board the size of Twickenham has possibilities.

With games like these, and many more still undreamt of, the sports news would no longer need to hide shyly at the back of the paper, nursing its inferiority complex in relation to political scandals and military coups. It could advance to its rightful place below the masthead, saving the readers the trouble of turning over thirty or so pages at breakfast to discover what really makes the world go round.

Too much sport indeed! There can never be too much.

No rest from tennis

Tennis is one of those sports in which I take an interest once a year. I think of Wimbledon as a stop on the District Line, but I like to know who have won the men's and women's singles, even if I do forget their names half an hour later.

Long ago I was an assistant racing tipster, with a sentimental preference for a horse called Gudmenarmist, which won at 33-1 the first time I selected it. Now, I look down the list of runners on Grand National day and Derby day, pick a horse with a likely name, and then make a point of finding out how – or if – it ran. But for the rest of the year racing does not exist for me.

Nor does rowing – bar the Boat Race. I might not sleep that Saturday night if I did not know who reached Mortlake first. And boxing did nothing for me until Cassius Marcellus Clay – "by his own admission," Alistair Cooke wrote, "the greatest man in the history of the human race" – came on the scene. I devoured every word of George Whiting about him in the *Evening Standard*. In fact, my interest in boxing can be said to have begun with the advent of Clay and ended with the retirement of Ali.

But to return to tennis. It has been a quiet game recently because John McEnroe has not been playing. Umpires and other officials have been able to relax, like battle-weary infantry temporarily resting behind the line, and a certain kind of spectator has stayed at home because, in their view, tennis without McEnroe incidents is a poor relation of tennis with them.

McEnroe and Ali are alike in a way. Both talk a lot, often loudly, but from the available evidence it is clear that Ali has a more flexible vocabulary and a more vivid imagination. Both would make a fortune at Speakers Corner, but I fancy that Ali would draw the bigger crowd.

I sometimes wonder how McEnroe would get on in a body-contact sport. If he can treat a dubious line call as a gross personal slander, what would he do if somebody trod on his head? It seems to me that he is usually so much better than his opponents that he could afford to ignore these little irritations, because he is going to win anyway.

But if we are having a rest from McEnroe, we are not having rest from tennis. We never do now. I have heard complaints that there is too much tennis, just as there is too much cricket, and despite being an ignoramus about tennis, I can well believe it.

I get the impression that, for example, every other town in

the United States has its own tournament and that the same players are forever playing each other. One week you open the paper and read that some superstar has won the Deadwood Gulch invitation classic; the next, that the superstar who was runner-up at Deadwood Gulch, fearing penury, has hurried across the prairie to win the Tombstone City pro-masters gold cup, beating the Deadwood champion in a "tie-break shoot-out".

If only it really were a shoot-out, in the OK corral style, how much more gripping it would be.

Scrabble's night of shame

I wonder when and where the next Night of Shame will be. Night of Shame always sounds to me like one of those "daring" and "explicit" films that turn out to be neither. At least a Night of Shame in sport can be real enough on its own level to make you feel a twinge of shame the morning after.

I have never witnessed one of those Nights of Shame that regularly get into the national news. This is because, although quite capable of roughing it, I am a stay-at-home by temperament and would rather not share the same train, plane, ferry or stadium with devotees of any sport who consider knives and bottles essential to a "good time".

But I have witnessed a Night of Shame in a suburban hall. I went to watch the final of a Scrabble championship, and there was carnage. Afterwards I felt I never wanted to play Scrabble again; and when a man reaches that pitch you know he has been shaken to his foundations.

P. G. Wodehouse wrote about policemen's helmets being stolen in Piccadilly on Boat Race night. What went on at the Scrabble final left that far behind in enormity. If the rival supporters of the finalists had had the chance they would not only have stolen every helmet in the Metropolitan Police, but also kidnapped the policemen underneath them.

Some of the supporters started causing trouble even before the Scrabble board had been ceremonially opened and the letter tiles placed ready. They arrived slightly tipsy, paid their entrance money with reluctance, if at all, and sat during the national anthem.

Yet the final itself passed off peacefully enough, as they say of marches, demonstrations and other bellicose assemblies at which thirty arrests are made instead of the expected five hundred. There were rude comments coming from the body of the hall, but nobody tried to assassinate the players.

It all began at the end with the announcement of the result. You would have thought a boxer who had lost every round had just been declared the winner.

The playing area was bombarded with rotten eggs and tomatoes and the players fled. The master of ceremonies who declared the result was dragged to the floor and debagged. A table stacked with tea-cups and saucers crashed over. Buns and cakes flew.

Somebody swung on a chandelier, plunging the hall into half-darkness. Women shrieked. Dogs howled. The fire alarm was set off. Windows were shattered and the curtains ripped down. Hot tea flowed across the floor. The rowdies fought with anyone they could lay hands on, including each other. Music started up: it was "Some Enchanted Evening" – the Howard Keel performance, I think (Strange how such a detail should register at such a time).

Order was not restored until well after midnight. In court next day, some of the accused said they could not remember a thing, and sentences were passed that most people considered lenient. A gentleman signing himself Ex-Scrabble Champion wrote to the local paper saying "Words fail me" and advocating horse-whipping for what he called "these mindless thugs who desecrated a great game."

In spite of suggestions to the contrary, the result of the final stood. The winner later announced his retirement from serious competition. The pressures, he explained, were too great, and in any case he wanted to give more time to his chrysanthemums.

So you see, after Scrabble's Night of Shame, how could I possibly be horrified at what mere football supporters do?

Carpet of daydreams

This is the age of the interview, especially in sport. I think it would be agreeable to be interviewed and often daydream about winning something, perhaps a trifle like a world championship, and then granting an audience to the press.

Imagine it, I have just won the world championship for – oh, anything will do, say carpet bowls. Cameras are clicking and flashing. Biros are being sucked. There am I at the centre of the universe for ten minutes, complete with business manager, wife, and delusions of grandeur. First question, please.

"What does it feel like to win the world title?"

"Great, just great. Unbelievable. I'm over the moon."

"How long have you been playing carpet bowls?"

"Ever since I was big enough to pick up a bowl – when I was two or three years old, I suppose."

"When did you win your first competition?"

"That's going back a bit, too. I think it was a Sunday school cup. I'd have been about nine then. I beat the clergyman's son in the final after morning service."

"Did you ever have coaching?"

"When I was old enough my father passed on a few wrinkles, as you might say. Otherwise I'm self-taught."

"Your father was a champion, wasn't he?"

"He was. Very shrewd player. My mother, too. They won the mixed pairs six years running at our local British Legion."

"What about your wife?"

"She makes sure I don't take it too seriously."

"And your sister?"

"She's a rebel; she prefers draughts."

"How often do you practise?"

"Most days, on the living-room carpet. Occasionally it's difficult fitting in practice with the telly, but so far we haven't come to blows, although we nearly did during Brideshead."

"And keeping fit?"

"I do Yoga, like David Bryant in the lawn game. Concentration's important if you're trying to avoid tables and chairs and a dog."

"Did you play at school?"

"There were no carpets there, I'm afraid."

"Is there an ideal carpet for your sort of bowling?"

"Wilton's as good as any. If the surface is too smooth the bowls tend to run in circles, which is confusing. I like a plain fawn carpet myself, no flowers or Cupids. I've known experienced players lose to novices because they played over flowers and Cupids. They lost motivation for some reason."

"Did you really think at the start of this championship that you would win it?"

"Well, if I hadn't thought so there wouldn't have been much point in going on."

"And in the final was there any time when you thought you were in real danger of losing?'

"Well, it was hard all the way, I suppose the worst moments for me were when I lost four shots on the twelfth and fifteenth ends. I got behind then and the pressure really built up."

"What were your thoughts before you delivered that fantastic winning bowl?"

"My mind was a total blank."

"Do you think carpet bowls will take off, like snooker and darts, as far as the public is concerned?"

"I hope so. It's got a lot in its favour. After all, it's cheap, you don't have to leave your living-room to play, and there's no crowd violence. It's pretty popular already in a quiet way – an excellent game for the long winter evenings. I think the Russians would enjoy it. As for the TV possibilities, carpet bowls couldn't be duller than many programmes, so by that token it must be in with a good chance of catching on."

"Do you see professionalism ever coming into the game?"

"If you can see professionalism coming into draughts you can see it coming into carpet bowls."

"What are your plans now?"

"I just want to relax for a week or so. It'll make a nice change to get off the carpet and on to the settee. You get a different angle on life from the settee, and there's less danger of cramp; it's like leaving the field to sit in the stand. After that I've got a promotional trip to the United States, and odds and ends like that."

"There's a strong rumour that you're going to write a book about the game – the definitive book."

"That's right. The game's got no literature yet. I want to spread the gospel. And I'll write every word of it myself. Do you think *Magic Carpet* would be a good title?"

The last question answered, the last hand shaken, the last compliment accepted, and the last orange juice drunk, I go home. I arrange the world championship shield on the living-room mantelpiece, not far from the Sunday school cup, agree with my wife that it is quite decorative but needs polishing, and remark that it has been a busy day.

At breakfast next morning I read about myself in the newspaper. There is not much to read. I wince: did I really say I was "over the moon"? I am also quoted as saying that the game will "take off", like snooker and darts, and as I spread marmalade on my second slice of toast I speculate that by the time that happens – if it ever does – I will have been long dead.

Passing glances

Rugby has interested me for almost as long as I can remember. Football I have followed from afar. Rugby people are supposed to know as little about football as footballers do about rugby but as a matter of fact I know a fair amount about football, superficially at any rate.

I am rather good at the name game. Ask me Scotland's Wembley Wizards forward line of 1928 and Jackson, Dunn, Gallacher, James and Morton will roll off my tongue like an incantation. Ask me the great Hibernian forward line of the 1950s and Smith, Johnstone, Reilly, Turnbull and Ormond will be a symphony in the ears of those who remember them.

And just to prove that I am not insular, did not Matthews, Taylor, Mortensen, Mudie and Perry help Blackpool win the FA Cup in 1953 and Jones, White, Smith, Allen and Dyson lead Tottenham Hotspur to the Cup and League double in 1960-61? You cannot ask about modern forward lines because there are none. There are only formations, which are not half so evocative.

I expect you would meet a blank stare if you played this little parlour game in reverse and asked a football follower to name back divisions. It would prove that the social differences between the games, though less marked than they used to be, are still an influence. Yet the Oxford University and Scotland

The Tottenham Hotspur team which won the FA Cup and League championship in 1961. Back row, left to right: Bill Brown, Peter Baker, Ron Henry, Danny Blanchflower, Maurice Norman, Dave Mackay, Bill Nicholson (manager). Front row, left to right: Cliff Jones, John White, Bobby Smith, Les Allen, Terry Dyson. (Photograph: Sport & General)

three-quarter line in 1925, Smith, Macpherson, Aitken and Wallace, were as fine and famous in rugby as the Wembley Wizards in football and the British Lions combination in 1971, Davies, Gibson, Dawes and Duckham, were as capable of magic as the Real Madrid of Puskas and di Stefano.

Social differences or no, the sport that holds you lifelong is more than likely to be the one you learnt at school. I went to a rugby-playing school but in our junior years, long before mini-rugby was thought of, we played football. I do not think I enjoyed the compulsory change, when we were about twelve, from football to rugby, at both of which I was a dunce, and it was a while before I nerved myself to the new, riskier and more complicated game. Some never do. Kevin Keegan has said that he played rugby in his youth but after many a manhandling "saw the light" and concentrated on football.

Between leaving school and entering real life – that is to say, in the British Army of the Rhine – I had three experiences of football. I was pressed into playing once, at Sennelager. When my unit were involved in some species of cup-tie I travelled by lorry to watch them lose at München Gladbach. Best of all, beside a radio in Berlin, I won a small bet that Blackpool would beat Bolton Wanderers in the 1953 FA Cup Final – a bet laid when Blackpool were 1–3 down with twenty minutes to go. Little wonder I remember Blackpool's forward line and that Mortensen scored three goals.

I have rarely gone to a football match just to pass the time. I needed a reason. Something special was at stake; it was an occasion beyond the norm, an eminent or legendary player was on view.

I have been at Highbury twice. The first time was in the late 1950s. Arsenal were playing Blackpool, for whom Matthews, in the evening of his career, was on the right wing. Doubtless there were others in the crowd that Saturday who, like me, came solely to see Matthews. I do not recollect that he did much, and even if he had done more the chances are I would not have appreciated it. It is strange how, knowing next to nothing of this or that art, we still go out of our way to watch the greatest artists as though we know a great deal.

Nor was my second visit to Highbury, about fifteen years later, specifically to see Arsenal. I wanted to see Best, Law and Charlton playing for Manchester United. Again I was deprived, which served me right for being a snob about names. Arsenal won 4–0 and for all that Best, Law and Charlton achieved I might have been watching a game on Hackney marshes.

When Crystal Palace played their first match in the first division Manchester United were the opposition and I crossed London to Selhurst Park. Best, Law and Charlton were less anonymous then and the result was 2–2, almost a triumph for Palace in the circumstances. I suppose I was lucky to get in and from the back of the dense crowd at the railway end I could catch only glimpses of the play between the heads and shoulders of spectators.

Probably the most significant match I have seen in the flesh was at White Hart Lane on a spring night in 1961. Tottenham, in the season of their Cup and League double, needed to beat Sheffield Wednesday to win the League. They did, 2–1. I think Wednesday scored first. Then, too, I was lucky to get in. North London was a foreign country to me at the time and Tottenham High Road on a night like that was no place for neutrals. I was condemned to an uttermost corner of the ground, high up.

Being a Scot, by birth if not conviction, I have seen Celtic and Rangers but never playing each other. I have also seen Raith Rovers, which is not so common. The only football match I ever reported was between Raith and, I fancy, Kilmarnock at Stark's Park, Kirkcaldy. My report, for a Scottish newspaper, was cut and rewritten beyond recognition.

5

Shakespeare
Started
Something

King Kong words

If you saw something described as great, brilliant, superb, glorious, breathtaking, awesome, stupendous, marvellous, amazing, unforgettable, magnificent, tremendous, stunning, devastating and fascinating, not to mention fantastic and incredible, what do you think it might be? One of the wonders of the world? A vision of the universe? The birth of a nation? The apocalypse?

If so, you would be wrong, and you can go and stand in a corner for your ignorance. Something far more momentous is being described – I mean Tom's goal and Jerry's try and Tweedledum's century and Tweedledee's return of service. With increasingly indiscriminate and hysterical emphasis, newspapers and commentators have been seeing sport in these terms for years, until the terms have lost meaning and become stock reactions, like a child's grab at a piece of chocolate.

Whenever I read or hear these words now, I recoil instinctively and tell myself, because I have seen and heard them a thousand times before, that in at least 999 cases they cannot be true. I do not object so much to the terms themselves: only to their over-use and misuse, to the piling of superlative on top of superlative, in accounts of events which in the heat of the moment may lure the scribbler into purple prose but next morning, or half an hour later, look rather grey.

Bernard Shaw said that all art criticism is a paraphrase of the man in the street's remark, "Pretty, ain't it?" Substitute "Good, ain't it?" and you have a paraphrase of the kind of sporting journalism I am talking about. I would in fact like to see the honourable old word, good, restored to favour, but there is scant chance of that.

It is not good enough for the media. It is not thought exciting enough. It sounds too like damning with faint praise. We are so conditioned to extravagant language in sport that if we see anything described as good we dismiss it with a sniff, telling ourselves that we want no truck with such dullness, and that we expect better from our heroes.

Which brings us to the villains without whom there would be no heroes. Things do go wrong in sport, and then a different vocabulary, just as tired, non-concrete and inappropriate, comes into play.

An own-goal in football is "tragic", a dropped catch in cricket "disastrous." Any kind of mistake is liable to be called "appalling" or "horrifying", as if hundreds died as a result. The same words are interchangeable and can be used on the ever more popular moral plane, apartheid, etc, where problems are always "dilemmas", and "concepts" and "imperatives" and "double standards" fill the reader's mind with fog.

While I am at it, I would also like to see the adverb put in its place – out of sight, for preference. Graham Greene has said it is a greater enemy of the writer than the adjective. It is almost always padding. "Sadly" and "happily" crop up most often.

"Sadly, he broke a leg in a tackle." And later: "Happily, he did not, as was at first feared, break his leg in the tackle." An example of running the gamut of emotion from A to B. One day I shall no longer be able to live because, sadly (or is it happily?), I shall be dead.

When I think of the "unforgettable" sporting occasions that I have completely forgotten, I sigh. To me, a goal is a goal and a century a century, no more, probably less. Watching one, I never undergo the mystical experiences that others apparently do. If I did, I would not stand the strain for long.

Breathtaking, magnificent, stupendous, and the rest of the heavyweights ought to be used sparingly, if at all. They are Hollywood words, straight from posters extolling *King Kong* and *Gone With The Wind*. They have all the impact now of a sponge.

Sweet quotations

There are fewer quotations on the sports pages than there used to be. That at least is my impression, probably connected with the fact that more sports are reported now and there is less space. Anyone tempted to resort to Shakespeare and Kipling, to mention only two favourites, knows that their words would be the first to go if cuts were needed – and quite right too, I say, in my capacity as a professional journalist.

It is a pity, all the same, that such quotations seem to be dwindling. They sweeten the tasteless lump of "objective" daily journalism. Note the inverted commas. I was interested to read, in his obituary, that James Cameron, who knew a thing or two about the business, scorned objectivity, realizing, no doubt, that attaining it is impossible until new technology takes over the writing as well as the printing of newspapers, thus rendering them unreadable.

A correspondent of this paper once began a cricket report with a poem of his own composition, which was immediately cut out. It was versatile of him, but he went over the score. If quotations, poetical ones in particular, must be used, sticking to the masters is better than writing your own.

By sticking to the masters I do not mean sticking to Shakespeare and Kipling. Far from it. Those two have been quoted to death anyway, besides which it is worth remembering that they are not to everyone's liking. No, I mean sticking to any author, good or bad, famous or obscure, whose books may be tracked down in the Charing Cross Road and its environs.

This gives the journalist wide scope as he brings his erudition into play. He can take his pick, from Aristotle to Zola, provided he gets his quotations right, which can be difficult, with only a few minutes in which to do his match report.

I like to quote – when I quote at all – from the smaller fry. Any schoolboy can quote from Shakespeare and Kipling, if not from Aristotle and Zola. Let them. My preference, reflecting to some extent my own reading habits, is for quoting from writers not read by a mass public.

Not long ago I quoted from Arthur Machen's *The London Adventure*. How many have heard of him? He was unknown to me until I happened to pick up his little book in a Regent Street shop. One fine day I may cull something from the Guernsey masterpiece by G. B. Edwards called *The Book of Ebenezer Le Page* (there are a few words about football in it), in the earnest hope of doing a service to others by encouraging them to read it, if they can spare the time from *Dynasty*.

A quotation should not only be apt. It should also make the reader blink, read it twice, and say to himself: "That's really good. I must try to get hold of the book." If it makes him or her forget the score and the result, so much the better, although that may be unreasonable.

Saki, Flann O'Brien, Jocelyn Brooke, James Agate, Max Beerbohm, Dorothy Parker, W. W. Jacobs, Philip Larkin, Stevie Smith – imagine how a few of their currants would improve the flavour of the next dumpling of a sports report you read.

Writing backwards

Bernard Levin once wrote his review of two Ionesco plays backwards because he did not understand them. Them understand not did he because backwards plays Ionesco two of review his wrote once Levin Bernard. That, I trust, makes it perfectly clear what he did.

There is wide scope for this approach in sport, much of which, in its technical aspects, is incomprehensible. Yes, you can say that of almost any subject, from skyscrapers to spiders, but here I am concerned with sport, whose language often totally baffles me – me, a sports journalist and therefore a supposed expert on every sport in the lexicon.

If it baffles me, then imagine its effect on the uninitiated reader, to whom it might come as a relief to turn to the back of his favourite newspaper and start reading the Arsenal report at the referee's name.

Technical language, beyond a necessary minimum, is a waste of space and, worse, a bore to read. Any skilled writer should be able to avoid it most of the time.

I am lucky because, without being an expert, I have a good knowledge of three or four sports – not enough to use a lot of technical verbiage but enough to see past it to the essentials. The players who read my stuff may miss something in consequence (for all I know they may miss everything), but I never write to impress them. The sort of reader I sub-consciously address myself to is somebody who was probably not at the match, could not care less about heavy technical considerations, but wants to be told, in simple English, what happened.

Take me away from the three or four sports I know and I would be as lost as Mr Levin at those plays. Tennis and motor racing would have me writing backwards at top speed. Tennis is reckoned to be one of those universal games, like football, that everybody intuitively understands, but you can include me out. Whenever by some miscalculation I see a snatch of it, I hear myself innocently saying "Great shot" to a stroke that cost the man who played it the set.

My attitude to motor racing was well expressed by an old colleague who said he always liked to know where it was on so that he would keep as far away as possible. It is a clanking paradise for those in love with technical language for its own sake. Again, as with tennis, everybody is supposed to understand, because everybody is supposed to spend six days of the week driving a car and the seventh cleaning it. But mention of nose cones and rear suspension mounting brackets would send my pen into reverse.

Reverse into pen my send would brackets mounting suspension rear and cones nose of mention . . . I am dropping a hint that you should now read this article backwards in order to discover its hidden beauties and subtleties.

Grub Street cake

As a journalist I have to speak with reluctant respect of clichés. I would be lost without them. Facts are the bricks with which newspapers are built, clichés the cement that binds them together. There are times when I congratulate myself that I never use clichés, but other times when, recognizing that some clichés are a matter of personal taste (one man's cliché is another man's happy turn of phrase), I realize that I probably use them as much as the next Grub Street loiterer.

Clichés are like the sense of humour. Just as everybody resents being accused of having no sense of humour, so they resent being accused of using clichés. And humour, too, is a matter of personal taste. If you slip and fall on a banana skin, half the world guffaws. The other half is sorry for your cuts and bruises.

In some newspaper offices there are notices warning reporters to avoid clichés like the plague. The people who put up the notices are fools. A journalist can no more avoid clichés than a sailor can avoid water. The best he can do is cut out as many as he can and try to disguise the rest by rephrasing. Or he can be reactionary and use plain English – but that is hard work and therefore unpopular.

Making no apologies for the preamble, I come at last to the subject of sport. Now sport is a minefield of cliché (if that itself is a cliché, I cannot help it). You can hardly step on a sentence without detonating one (and if that is a mixed metaphor, I cannot help it, either). In plain English, you cannot say a thing that has not been said a million times already – which raises the problem of how to say it as though it were new yesterday.

Consider the reports of rugby matches. You go along to Richmond and, if you are lucky, you see three or four tries scored. A wing runs from his own half to score beside the corner flag. Thinking to add colour, the reporter says that "he pinned his ears back", "ran like the wind", "showed the opposition a clean pair of heels".

These are clichés – or are they? It depends on whether you are sensitive to imagery, however faded. The phrases may not register with you at all, which could be proof that they are clichés. I am sure that over the years I have had a wing "running like the wind" or "showing the opposition a clean pair of heels", but I am prepared to swear with my last breath that I have never had him "pinning his ears back". Of that I am guiltless. I now prefer to say merely that X scored a try, and, if he ran from his own half, to mention the fact in precisely those words, leaving the reader to draw his own mental picture, if he so wishes, of the not uncommon spectacle of a man running.

Let us linger at Richmond. In the same match the full back of the winning team, having scored a few points – "a hatful of points"? – adds a dropped goal to his total in the last minute – "the dying minutes". This may be referred to as "the icing on the cake" or even as "the icing on his personal cake". I am fond of cake, but this one is too mouldy for words. And, equally fond though I am of Westerns, I consider "another scalp to hang on their belts" a dead way of saying "another victory".

But then, I may be in the minority. Ears, heels, hats, cakes and scalps, used together – "thrown into the melting pot"? – may be the stuff of which living English is made. As I said, some clichés are a matter of personal taste. If nothing else, the writers who use them have the courage of their clichés.

Painting the weed

Shaftesbury Avenue is a long way from Wembley and Wimbledon and yet we sports journalists should feel at home in it. I am thinking of all those inflated adjectives up there in lights – brilliant this, magnificent that, unforgettable something else. Substitute a goal or a race for a new Pinter or an old Rattigan and you would not know the difference.

The words are tired, and so am I of seeing them, wherever they are. More than that, I do not believe them most of the time. That play, I think, as I walk down Shaftesbury Avenue, will probably close in six weeks, despite the breathless assurances of the critics that it is a milestone and a masterpiece.

Where will the brilliance and magnificence and unforgettableness be then? And, by the same token, what of the brilliance and magnificence and unforgettableness of some sporting performance that lasts, not six weeks, but six seconds?

We were in the foyer of the National Theatre the other evening and found ourselves at the same table as a young man and a girl who were, my wife assured me, typical Sloane Rangers. The young man had lately visited China and the girl asked what he thought of it. "It was raining and there was a cold wind," was all he said.

So much for China. The girl changed the subject to Kensington, evidently wishing to hear no more of a country where they actually have such frightfully boring things as horrid rain and wind.

That dialogue confirmed me in my preference for Texas as opposed to Sloane Rangers, but that is by the way. What is not by the way is the moral to be drawn from it.

The young man was, for a moment, an unwitting, unpaid

critic of China, a big subject that he covered in a few words of biblical brevity. Would that all critics, of the theatre, sport or anything else, were as hard to impress as he and not given to painting the weed rather than the lily, mechanically churning out words like brilliant, magnificent and unforgettable about the routine, the average and the everyday.

I forget what we had gone to see at the National, but it was not *Pravda*, which is about a newspaper editor and his proprietor. Nearly all Fleet Street novels and plays are about the bosses. What we need, to correct the balance, are more works about sports hacks. They do not have to be brilliant, magnificent and unforgettable – just good of their kind (which *Hold the Back Page!* reportedly is not).

And if the authors want to add a touch of breathtaking originality, avoid the biggest cliché in the genre, and give their stuff a semblance of truth to life, I suggest they make the hacks happily married and without a drink problem.

Elementary sport

Sport is all about winning, or so the experts tell us. Tweedledum beats Tweedledee and nothing could be plainer than that, you might think. But in sport, as in real life, appearances are deceptive: how deceptive you do not know until you have worked as a newspaper sub-editor.

Most writing about sport, like most writing about love, consists of saying the same things, stating a few elementary truths, over and over again. The best of it artfully conceals this repetition and persuades you, for a moment, that what you are reading over breakfast is as fresh as hilltop air.

Tweedledum beating Tweedledee is the most elementary truth of all. It can be contained in one line of small type or expanded to a column of florid prose. There are times when you wish there was more than one line, if you happen to be interested in the subject; and there are times, believe it or not, when the prose is so bad that you would readily exchange the eight hundred words for the one line.

Now Tweedledum beating Tweedledee is a straightforward matter at Wimbledon, Wembley or Watford. But cross the Atlantic and complications set in. Sub-editors know this. They handle copy from American news agencies every day and in lists of tennis results it is full of synonyms for beat and defeated. Beat and defeated are used at the start, as a gesture to dull tradition, but soon give way to brasher verbs. Tweedledum can not only beat, defeat or roll over Tweedledee; he can also blank, edge, blast, upset, put down, sweep past or sideline him.

Naturally, the sensitive eyes of English readers are protected from such barbarous evasions. Down comes the blue pencil or black biro, and beat or defeated takes its rightful place between subject and object, with the occasional upset or edge as variation – more by accident than design.

It just goes to show, once again, that Bernard Shaw was right when he said that England and America were two nations separated by a common language.

Underworld of print

Myles na Gopaleen, the great *Irish Times* columnist, compiled what he called a "Catechism of Cliché . . . A harrowing survey of sub-literature and all that is pseudo, mal-dicted and calloused in the underworld of print." Here is a simple sample:

"What happens to blows at a council meeting?
It looks as if they might be exchanged.
What does pandemonium do?
It breaks loose.
Describe its subsequent dominion.
It reigns.
How are allegations dealt with?
They are denied.
Yes, but then you are weakening, sir. Come now, how are they denied?
Hotly.
What is the mean temperature of an altercation, then?
Heated.
What is the behaviour of a heated altercation?
It follows.
What happens to order?
It is restored.
Alternatively, in what does the meeting break up?
Disorder.
What does the meeting do in disorder?
Breaks up.
In what direction does the meeting break in disorder?
Up.
In what direction should I shut?
Up."

And here is my contribution:
Over which heavenly body do footballers fly when ecstatic?
The moon.
What is every game, from bridge to football, alleged to be all about?
Pressure.
Give one non-clinical synonym for injury.

Knock.

How does a player get a knock?

He suffers or sustains it.

And having suffered or sustained a knock, what does the luckless fellow do with it?

He carries it.

In his hip pocket?

No, in his right hand – or left, if he is peculiar.

What chance is a goalkeeper given by a fierce shot from a range of nine inches?

No.

Of which two equal mathematical parts do matches consist, some more than others? Take your time before replying: this is a very difficult question.

Halves.

Excellent. In which direction does the curtain move when the season begins?

Up.

And when it ends?

Down.

But come, please, does the football season ever end?

No.

So why drag the curtain into it? Why not leave it permanently up and save the stage-hand unnecessary exertion?

That is something to be borne in mind.

It would also, would it not, rid us of the temptation to compare the start of the season with the dawn, since we are agreed there is no dusk, and you cannot have the one without the other?

Precisely.

A stage too far

Shakespeare started something when he said that all the world's a stage. He started a cliché which has rolled down the centuries and landed on the sports pages with a dull thud.

Now, all the field's a stage. The curtain goes up/rings up/rises/lifts on a new season/act/scene. The actors/players are learning their parts/training, so that when the call/cue/time comes to leave the dressing room/changing room/pavilion and walk/trot/run on to the stage/field/court, they will be word-perfect/fit for the drama/tragedy/comedy/match that follows.

In the wings hover the prompters/trainers and the directors/managers/coaches. In front or round about are assembled the audience/spectators/crowd. Among them, but boxed in (for their own safety?), sit the critics/reporters/media, primed with Thespian allusions, and ready to pounce on the smallest faults in ensemble/teamwork or interpretation/tactics.

Have I omitted anything from the repertory? I expect so. But then, even the finest actors suffer lapses of memory, just as the finest sportsmen have the odd bad game.

Seriously – and sport is serious, isn't it? – we are overdue a change of simile. Better still would be no simile at all. I know Wembley and Wimbledon and Twickenham and Epsom and Lord's and St Andrews are stages at least as great as the Olivier and the Old Vic. I know they have plays and players there at least as great as *Hamlet* and Scofield. But I do not want to be told so any more. I want to know where I am – to be told that Twickenham is Twickenham and Lord's is Lord's. I know both too well to mistake them for the West End.

Exit the stage simile, I say. Banish it from the boards. Boo and hiss it to death. It has had a long run since its first night – a run about twelve times that of *The Mousetrap*. Time to end the ovation, turn off the lights, bring down the curtain, eat the last chocolate, and catch a taxi home. In the morning you may read Irving Wardle, but not on the same page as the football results.

All in the mind

It is a question Jung and Freud used to ask themselves: "I wonder what is going through the young man's mind at this moment?" They asked it with a serious purpose and because they were professionally curious. The television sports commentator asks it – aloud – because he has fallen into a silly habit.

You do not have to watch television every day or every week to hear that question. It is asked so often that, no matter how selectively you watch, you cannot avoid it.

Perhaps it occurs in every commentary. To find out – and I believe it would be worth finding out – somebody ought to watch all televised sport during a heavy month and keep a record. Being a viewer so selective as hardly to be counted a viewer at all by current standards, I would sooner die than volunteer for the job, and perhaps we should wait until the Olympic Games for such an experiment. Hammer throwers always have plenty going through their minds. The commentators will have a field day.

The point about the question is that there is no point. The commentator does not need to ask it because nine, probably ten, times out of ten he knows, we know, and any fool knows or can guess what is going through the mind concerned, however expressionless the face.

Sport, after all, consists of a few basic experiences and emotions, endlessly repeated. There is nothing intellectual or metaphysical about it.

You win, you lose; you succeed, you fail; you play well, you play badly; you like, you dislike; you feel high, you feel low. Simple. When a goalkeeper loses a match by letting the ball through his legs in extra time, you need little imagination to know what is going through his mind, and that it is not fit for mixed company.

On happy occasions the question is the same. A golfer wins the Open by holing a thirty-foot putt across the eighteenth green at St Andrews. From the box come the lugubrious words of the amateur psychologist: "I wonder what is going through his mind now . . ."

One look at the champion's face and demeanor, one moment of putting yourself in his shoes, would tell you, if you are backward enough to need telling. Then again, such is the nature of the pleasure, his mind is probably blank. Jung and Freud would have understood.

A linguistic athlete

"I could make a deaf stockbroker read my pages on music", Bernard Shaw declared of his time as a professional critic, and in doing so summed up his own readability on everything. I have read him with pleasure on income tax, which is about as warm a tribute as you could pay to any writer, and I would have read him with delight on sport if he had ever written about it, for he was a highly trained athlete of language.

Shaw was undoubtedly a great journalist-critic and there-fore, by definition, a great columnist. I would not mind if I never saw another of his plays but, as a journalist, I would not like to be without his music and theatre reviews, all eight volumes. One of their cardinal attractions is that they are not always about Covent Garden and Drury Lane. Shaw often took his eye off the ball. He knew the value of digression, and you are as likely to read in his pages about doctors and soldiers as you are about singers and actors. There is even an interview with a pianist in which Shaw, although he undertook the assignment reluctantly – "I would not wish to intrude on so fine and noble a lady in the ribald character of a journalist" – demonstrated that the best interview should reveal almost as much of the writer as of the subject.

You will also find references to prize-fighting and cycling. Shaw had no interest in sport as such. "Cricket", he said, "save in its humorous, brief, and only tolerable form of tip and run, is a grosser bore than anything else except football."

But boxing appealed to him; he was an amateur boxer in his early days in London; and in his maturity he formed a notable friendship with Gene Tunney. His first attempt to ride a bicycle was on Beachy Head, watched by coastguards, who were so amused by his efforts that he wished the audiences for his plays laughed as much.

He said that Mozart taught him how to say profound things and at the same time remain flippant and lively. This is not the place for the profundity, real or imagined, but it is worth ending this long and unashamed digression from sport with a few of the flippancies from the reviews, to suggest the man and the tone:

"I do not smoke, do not drink, and feel like a pickpocket whenever circumstances compel me to lounge."

"There is nothing that soothes me more after a long and maddening course of pianoforte recitals than to sit and have my teeth drilled by a finely skilled hand."

"The other evening, feeling rather in want of a headache, I bethought me that I had not been to a music hall for a long time."

"The most important event in the musical world since my last article, from my point of view, has been the influenza catching me, or, as my friends preposterously insist on putting it, my catching the influenza."

"The man (a cornet soloist outside a public house) played with great taste and pathos; but, to my surprise, he had no knowledge of musical etiquette, for when, on his holding his hat to me for a donation, I explained that I was a member of the Press, he still seemed to expect me to pay for my entertainment."

"It is all work and no play in the brain department that makes John Bull such an uncommonly dull boy."

Don't read on?

I know somebody who never reads newspaper reports which use the word set in a certain way in the headline. Set in the tennis sense, yes, but not when it means ready, as in Spurs Striker Set for Comeback.

I would not carry my dislike of certain words, or their misuse, to that length, yet I can understand the view of a particular word in headlines as a sort of warning signal about the probable tediousness of the stuff below.

Package is, I think, another example. Package is used so often now that Christmas seems to be going on all the year round, except that the packages do not contain longed-for gifts but measures to combat national problems such as football hooliganism. The measures have little chance of implementation, let alone success, but the packages, the wrappings, have the bright colouring of optimism and soothe the social conscience.

A package of measures is usually described as being launched – another vogue word, another warning signal saying to you: "Don't read on." How packages can be launched is a mystery. Messages have been put in bottles and thrown into the sea, bobbing ashore years later on the other side of the world. They, if you like, were launched. But packages weighed down with measures would soon sink.

Not that the measures would be missed; the sea-bed is as good a resting place as any for them, and at least the paper they were written on might be useful as food for fish. The only danger would be indigestion.

Indigestion is what a monstrosity of a word like prestigious causes. The people who launch packages of measures consider their work prestigious. The Queen and Mrs Thatcher and the Minister for Sport occupy prestigious positions. The FA Cup is a prestigious trophy. I am writing this in a prestigious newspaper. Berkeley Square is in a prestigious part of London and the nightingale that sang there is a more prestigious bird than the sparrow.

After pronouncing prestigious seven times in rapid succession, as above, and then rearranging your lips back into their normal shape, you may agree with me about the indigestion. Perhaps indigestion is a prestigious complaint. Certainly a prestigious trade union leader seemed to be suffering from the verbal variety when he said, not that his members had been given a time limit in pay negotiations, but that they were "locked into a predetermined time frame." I reckon he was saying it the prestigious way.

Call them hooligans

Going home in the train at midnight from Victoria I fell to thinking about football fans. It was an appropriate place to think about them because it is in trains that the worst of the fans get up to their most malevolent mischief.

Be not afraid. I am not going to mount a moral high horse. It would certainly unseat me. As a wordsmith of sorts I am more interested in the usual descriptions of these fans – "mindless louts", "yobbos", "hooligans", "drunken idiots", "scum", "wild animals", "morons", "cowards", and "madmen". I want to suggest that one or two of these terms go a little over the top, even about fans at their worst.

"Hooligans" is all right. The Oxford Dictionary defines a hooligan as "one of a gang of young street roughs". My dictionary is not modern enough to contain "yobbo", but I imagine that "yobbos" and "hooligans" are offspring of the same parents.

"Cowards" is permissible, too, though with reservations. But "scum" and "wild animals" are not. Human beings are not scum, whatever your opinion in the heat of the moment, and the wildness of animals, unlike the behaviour of some fans, is natural and practical.

As for "mindless louts", which is the most frequent description of all, it may come as a surprise to those who use it – as it did to me – to find that "lout" means "awkward fellow, bumpkin, clown" – in short a harmless person, which a fan on the rampage is not. Attaching "mindless" to the noun is mere snobbery. (Incidentally, I remember "mindless" being excised from a caption on the sports pages because the photograph was so clear that the fans could have identified themselves, and it was suggested that the word might have been defamatory.)

Please do not rush into indignant correspondence telling me about your terrible experiences of football hooligans, asking me if I have ever suffered at their hands, and accusing me of defending them. I admit I have had no experiences of that kind, and I am not defending football hooligans. What I am trying to defend is the language. I am making a simple plea to cut out the Blimpish vituperation, call them hooligans, and leave it at that.

Coming to a head

Arthur Christiansen, a revered editor of the *Daily Express* wrote a book called *Headlines All My Life*. I too have worked in the headline factory a long time, but I am chary of boasting about it because few headlines are taken in, let alone remembered, by the public.

The best headline I ever wrote was not printed, which may have coloured my subsequent attitude, besides ensuring that I could not forget it. It was for a preview in a weekly newspaper of a film about a herd of bulls running wild on board a cargo boat, and it read:

DILEMMA WITH HORNS

I thought it perfect then, and still think so, nearly thirty years after creating it in pain and blood. The editor, silly man, rejected it. Only personal exposure to the bulls thundering around that boat as though it were a china shop would, I feel, have changed his mind for him.

My favourite headline now is:

TODAY'S FIXTURES

It is unlikely to make the reader gasp in admiration or laugh, but it is clear, concise and cannot be faulted factually or grammatically. I enjoy writing it because I do not have to think about it and can therefore devote much more time to the text below, which in any case is all that matters. A headline, gaudy or plain, is but the label on the packet. Journalists call a dull headline a label. Yet there is a sense in which a label is the best headline. You cannot mistake its meaning.

But I can still appreciate a clever headline when I see one. I am not blind to apt imagination, subtle word-play or a good pun, even after years of my own attempts – good, bad or indifferent, mostly indifferent – to ape the masters of a curious craft. If I have a rule-of-thumb, it is that spontaneity is almost everything. Strain too long after the "bright" headline and it will probably not come, or if it does it will be slow and sound contrived.

When West Indies were bowled out for a small score in a Test match, an Australian paper celebrated the event in letters as tall as stumps:

CALYPSO COLLAPSO

When Karam, the Wellington and All Blacks full back, kicked five penalty goals against Wales at Cardiff, a Sunday paper headline proclaimed:

DAY OF THE WELLINGTON BOOT

A Scottish victory over Spain at Hampden Park long ago, in

which a certain Blackpool forward played a decisive part, was summed up thus:

MUDIE SCUPPERS THE ARMADA

Two fruitless high balls into the penalty area by the losing side near the end of an English league match inspired some anonymous desk man late in the evening to write:

TWO CROSSES COME TO NOUGHT

Etc. Ad infinitum. Of the writing of ingenious headlines there is no end. One day there may be a headline of the year award to go with the rest of the media's passports to immortality.

But ingenuity is not all. I like the story Cardus tells of suggesting to the sub-editors that they might try to vary the headline on his reports occasionally; he did not see why, however true, it so often had to be:

STEADY BATTING BY LANCASHIRE

They took the hint and next day, or soon after, their deeply pondered alternative appeared at the top of the page:

SOLID BATTING BY LANCASHIRE

If you dig back far enough into the files of *The Times*, you will find, on pages devoid of illustration, headlines of self-effacing size and content saying things like:

GOLF:
THE OPEN CHAMPIONSHIP
COTTON WINS AGAIN

Think how such a feat would be treated now. We have come a long way since headlines of that kind. Or have we?

6

A
Bowler's
Summer, 1994

May

Sunday 1

I see that today is the birthday of Joseph Heller, who wrote *Catch-22*; of Sir Bob Reid, chairman of British Rail; and of Una Stubbs, the actress. It is also the anniversary of the birth of the Duke of Wellington, of the death of David Livingstone and Josef Goebbels, and of the Union of England and Scotland. Of more pressing concern to many thousands of people all over Britain, it is the opening day of the bowls season, and the sun is shining, though probably not for long.

My club had its first roll-up two evenings ago, but for me grass does not take over from carpet until May has begun. The indoor season came to an end last week and I collected yet another runner's-up medal in the afternoon league at Croydon. This time we were second on shots difference, and as usual we looked back at our last few matches, identifying the silly loss to a "weaker" team that, had it been a win, would have made us champions. But no more post-mortems, if you please.

This afternoon we were at Brockham for tea on the church lawn, a regular indulgence, and afterwards we found the bowling club, four rinks, set on a sort of plateau among trees, where they were playing Handcross from Sussex. A nicer start to the season could hardly be imagined.

Tuesday 3

Still not on the green yet. I've just finished reading Angelica Garnett's book on the Bloomsbury set, *Deceived With Kindness*, and came across this, about an afternoon at Rodmell:

> When the meal was over we all trooped into the garden, invited by Leonard (Woolf) to play the ritual game of bowls. If the first half of the entertainment had been Virginia's, the second was his. He took charge of the game, pressing everyone to play, even the least experienced, who were given handicaps and praised if they did better than expected. Leonard paced the doubtful distances with large, thick-soled feet placed carefully one before the other . . . Leonard's word was law, his judgement final, and we would continue with the gentle, decorous game while he carried on a discussion with Julian or Quentin about the habits of animals or local politics.

Interesting to discover the well-known people who have played the game, or had some connection with it. I once heard that Douglas Hurd played, and wrote asking for an interview; he replied that he didn't think being an honorary vice-president of the West Witney club, or some such, entitled him to speak of bowls.

Sunday 8

To Worthing, my spiritual home, for the first time this season – or rather, to Ferring, where we had fish and chips at the Lemon Tree Cafe, walked inland along the river bank, round the houses, past the little war memorial, and back by the greensward on the edge of the beach. A Tory heartland here, though more of a heartattackland after the local election results.

Deciding it was too early to go home, we drove to Beach House Park, which looked its spring best. Players, all in white, men and women, were dispersing after a match; the flowers in their boxes stood up straight and glowing. We sat with our tea outside the Bowl Inn, where the grass was fresh and green, and I thought: by September there'll be no grass left, trodden into mud and dust by ten thousand pairs of shoes. I thought, too, of Pat Sullivan, reckoning it to be little more than ten years since I first met him in the press room there. Now he's gone. They ought to name that room after him, or put up a plaque. But then, you could make a case for doing the same in Jimmy Jones's memory. Let the neutrality of the press be observed.

Wednesday 11

At last! – a roll-up, alone; one toucher in about ten ends. The Wallington green is closer cut than it usually is in the second week of the season. I scanned the notice-board; noted competition dates and opponents; cleared my pigeon-hole of fixture booklet, membership card, captain's exhorting letter; struggled to work the new combination lock on the club's main door. All that done, felt ready for another summer, my twenty-second in this blessed game.

Saturday 14

A wet afternoon, part of which I spent looking through my collection of bowls books. There are twenty-five of them and I'm proud that only four are exclusively instructional. As with golf ("Groove Your Swing My Way", etc), so with bowls. There are too many instructional books and too few that can be read purely for pleasure. The instruction all boils down to a few basic points: only the author's name is different. Reading a book by Jack Nicklaus won't enable you to play golf as well as he does, any more than reading a book by Tony Allcock will make you bowl like him; yet the publication of these books mischievously implies that such miracles are possible.

The first book on bowls that I bought – at Hatchards in Piccadilly, I recall – was *Bryant on Bowls*, the 1970 edition. There's almost a biblical feel to it now, coming as it did from the world's most famous player, before Allcock and others had been heard of.

Wednesday 18

London Scottish versus the Civil Service at Mansfield, a club I thought rather inaccessible, until someone advised me to take the Underground to Kentish Town, catch the C2 or 214 bus to William Ellis School, and walk a short distance up Croftdown Road. Simple. Did I hear some car-obsessed person snort? Well, I've heard motorists, too, describe the difficulties they had finding Mansfield, in the network of streets between Dartmouth Park Hill and Highgate Road. I used to approach it from the Dartmouth Park Hill side; now I know better.

The Scottish lost by a lot. Afterwards, the C2 again, and I rode through London on an evening of late spring – Camden Town, Regent's Park, Great Portland Street, among my old haunts. I have now lived almost as long in south London as I did in north, but it is on evenings like this, with the city poised for summer, that I wish I was a "northerner" again. Can't explain it further.

Saturday 21

Sussex versus London Scottish at Henfield. It rained most of the time, and I couldn't get up on the sodden green, until it dried a little towards the finish. My worst end: one in the ditch, one on the edge, one wrong bias (my rink played as a triple because our skip failed to appear). We dropped six on that end. My best end? Can't remember. Perhaps there wasn't one. Alex Colquhoun, the Scottish vice-president, gave me a lift to Caterham after the game, passing a nasty accident involving three cars on the M23, and from Caterham I got home to Carshalton by train.

Tuesday 24

Sheila Sullivan, Pat's widow, has been disposing of his bowls library and she sends me *The Modern Technique of Bowls*, by H. P. Webber and Dr J. W. Fisher, both Devon men. Yet another instructional book! – but no matter. Harold Webber was EBA singles champion in 1925, and Jack Fisher was a good bowler too; he was also a specialist in mental health, which knowledge might be an asset on the green when temperament enters the equation.

J. P. Monro's *Bowls Encyclopaedia*, published in Australia over forty years ago, was not in Pat's collection and I've asked Booksearch at Hay-on-Wye to see what they can do. Godfrey Bolsover, who compiled his own encyclopaedia, described Monro's death in 1958 as "a grievous loss to bowls and literature." Most of Pat's books have gone to the EBA in Worthing. Incidentally, somebody had to consult Bolsover's tome at Wallington the other day, remarking, "It's bigger than the Bible." "And more interesting," I suggested with a straight face.

Monday 30

Ruth sends me from Aberdeen a newspaper cutting about a retired farmer who's built a three-rink bowling green in his back garden at Turriff. It took him four years. He says there were five trees and a hedge in the garden and the soil was heavy clay, little use for gardening.

June

Friday 3

Lost in the first round of the handicap singles, which may be the first time such a thing has happened to me – not the loss, I mean, but the earliness of it, and in that of all competitions. The score was 21–20. I lay match at 20–18 when he moved the jack for three shots – and I had back woods. But I wouldn't have deserved to win anyway; my play was all over the shop. Could be age.

With almost no work, May was a barren month for me, and I turned over the calendar page with relief. The Middleton Cup starts tomorrow and I'm going to watch Surrey play Oxfordshire at Croydon. On Sunday there's a D-Day commemorative mixed fours beside the Solent, on the Southsea Castle greens. Later in the month, to Llandrindod Wells for the women's international series and British Isles championships. I'm told it's a beautiful place, which is an even better reason for going there than the bowls. Besides, my knowledge of Wales has been restricted, so far, to the south.

My sister-in-law and her granddaughter have been up from Devon while Joy was visiting friends at Morfa Nefyn, across the water from Anglesey, and I showed the girl a bowl. She was surprised at its smallness. "The bowls look much bigger on TV," she said. And they say the camera doesn't lie.

Sunday 5

Portsmouth swarming with people and tinkling with medals for the D-Day commemoration. The mixed fours was won by two husbands and their wives from the Pagham club at Bognor Regis. No D-Day veterans in the final, nor in the previous rounds, as far as I could ascertain, but I spoke to onlookers who had been in the first wave on the Normandy beaches. One, Bill Lamb, from Broxburn, had been with the Royal Signals, going in immediately behind the Canadians; another, whose name I didn't catch, was in Combined Operations – he ended the war in Singapore, having been with the invasion force rendered superfluous by the dropping of the atomic bombs.

Tom Snape, an ex-Marine from Liverpool, devised the competition. He and his wife, Pat, drove me to Portsmouth Harbour station afterwards, and I left them with the idle thought that something similar might be got up for the seventy-fifth anniversary of D-Day. He and I will be – may be – in our early eighties by then.

Stopped for an evening meal at Clapham Junction. As usual, had to walk only a few steps to a Pizza Hut and a McDonald's. Passed both with distaste, turned into the Northcote Road, and, first right, found a very tolerable tapas bar.

Didn't go to Croydon after all for Surrey's Middleton Cup match. Too wet. Watched the South Africa-England rugby on TV instead.

Wednesday 8

Joy and I play a game over breakfast in which she asks me to guess the ages of people in *The Times* birthdays. This morning I was many years wrong with Norma Shaw (and all the bowlers' ages given by the paper were supplied by me) but spot-on with Derek Underwood – just like his bowling.

Wednesday 15

The London Scottish Bowling Association has produced a booklet to mark its seventy-fifth anniversary, and I note that six members have won the EBA singles, from Jimmy Carruthers in 1905, the championship's first year, to Andy Thomson in 1981. Not a bad record.

Mowed the grass in the morning, played twenty-one ends in the afternoon, only a roll-up, and then treated myself to a circular tour of south London. The 157 bus from Wallington to Crystal Palace; the 3 from Crystal Palace to Trafalgar Square; the 176 from Charing Cross Road to Waterloo (a girl on the seat in front of me was writing a poem called "His Desires'); the Underground from Waterloo to Morden; the 157 to Carshalton ponds. How leafy and green, unexpectedly so, are parts of Crystal Palace and Sydenham and Dulwich. What value is a one-day travel card.

Felt pleasantly relaxed after all this. I'm not one to complain about feeling tired; that's what a body's for. Others seem to regard tiredness as a personal insult.

There was a rail strike today and my travels should be seen in that context. Was slightly alarmed when I saw a newspaper placard, "Hundreds trapped in Kennington Tube derailment," but encountered no delays. Refreshments on the South Bank (the umpteenth time), then browsed along the tables outside the National Film Theatre – one of the best selections of second-hand books, particularly paperbacks, in London. Acquired *Dead As Doornails*, Anthony Cronin's account of bohemian life in Dublin, Soho and Paris forty years ago. Am I a frustrated bohemian? A bohemian bowler! It's almost a contradiction in terms.

Saturday 18

"What a lovely day," Joy said in the evening. "Yes, it was," I said, in the melancholy of the past tense. We'd been to

Worthing, where Hampshire beat Sussex in the Middleton Cup at the Pavilion club. On the verandah I saw Jimmy Elms, based in Bournemouth when he was secretary of the EBA but now living in Worthing. "You've got dual nationality today," I suggested to him. "I don't mind who wins so long as it's Hampshire," he replied. I also spoke to Ian Keat, the Hampshire secretary; he seemed taller than ever, and I said so, with the rider that perhaps this was only because I had become shorter.

Kept up with the Lord's Test match on TV in the pavilion. Gordon Cummings, the Sussex president, was doing the same. "Cricket," he declared, "is the best game God ever invented. It's one man against eleven." "And the umpires," I added.

Monday 20

We have a local afternoon triples league known as the Tons, owing to the fact that some of the competing clubs have names ending in -ton – Carshalton, Sutton, Cuddington, and so on. Wallington started it years ago, mainly for the benefit of retired men, and have never won it.

It introduces you to some characters. Once, over our tea and biscuits, an opponent told us he had played in Glenn Miller's band – the saxophone, I think – in North Africa during the war, and that when members of the band heard Miller was dead, they cheered. This same bowler had played in other bands under the likes of Eric Winstone, Harry Roy and Joe Loss, and I asked him who in his opinion was the best, and he answered, "Joe Loss."

Interviewed Paul Vamvacopoulos at his home in Sutton in the evening. A good idea, it seemed to me, since there are very few Greek bowlers in England and even fewer in Greece. I had the impression of a disappointed man – disappointed because the England selectors had continually overlooked him. But then, as far as that's concerned, he cannot be in a category of one.

Monday 23

Llandrindod Wells. The journey began badly. The ticket office at Carshalton was shut, and the clerk at Victoria gave me a ticket to Llandudno – an error attributable to his Asian background, my Scottish accent (slight or non-existent to a Scot, strong to anyone else), and the Welsh name. They sorted it out at Paddington.

After changing at Swansea, a lovely leisurely run to Llandrindod, on the Heart of Wales line, the stations having familiar names such as Llanelli, Ammanford, Llandeilo and Llandovery. The Rock Park amphitheatre in Llandrindod is a wonderful setting for the game, possibly the finest in Britain. A raised clubhouse in Swiss style, two greens on one level, a third lower down, trees everywhere and the Radnorshire hills rising and falling in the distance – the hills that I see from my bedroom as I write this. Suggested to club members that they sell photographs of the view. Better than club badges.

Saturday 25

In the hallway of my guest-house in Tremont Road is printed this place-name that many have heard of but few can pronounce:

Llanfairpwllgwyngyllgogerychwyrndrobwll-llantysiliogogogoch

plus the translation:

St Mary's Church, in a Dell of White Hazel Trees, near the Rapid Whirlpool, by the Red Cave of the Church of St Tysilio.

If you're contemplating going there, it's in Anglesey.

Won a raffle prize at Rock Park, a box of Newberry Fruits. These days I'm having more luck with raffles than I'm having on the green.

Monday 27

The bowls ended at midday and I spent the afternoon in Builth Wells, a compact town beside the Wye. I'd not been there before but remembered the name from an encounter in Church Stretton in Shropshire years ago. We were having our Saturday evening meal in the King's Arms and got into conversation with two women, one of whom had a card, "Best of Breed", fastened to a bosom big enough to have accommodated a dozen cards. They were returning with their whippets from the Builth Wells dog show.

Should have mentioned earlier that David Rhys Jones, Anne Dunwoodie and I represented the press at the bowls, but might as well have stayed at home, for all the space we were given. Hairstyles and rent-boys at the World Cup were deemed more important, by the *Daily Telegraph* at least. So much for sport.

July

Monday 4

The lady who runs the guest-house where I'm staying on Prestwick Road in Ayr comes from Braemar. Thought her accent sounded more north-eastern than south-western. Nothing like a familiar intonation for putting you at your ease. I stayed with her a few years ago but don't recall her Grampian roots. Then, Ayr and miles around were bracing themselves for the Open golf, at, I think, Troon; this year it's at Turnberry. The railway line from Glasgow to Ayr is an unrolling film of seaside links, experiencing which makes me wish I had persevered with long-ago golf lessons instead of giving up for the possibly irrelevant reason that I couldn't hit the ball straight.

Rain poured for much of the first day of the British Isles

championships on the Northfield greens. Also it got colder and colder. And to think that when I left London twenty-four hours earlier people were praying for a break in the heat and humidity. The rain crept into the press cabin. I was glad to escape at close of play and meet my sister Ruth, down from Aberdeen until Friday; she's staying on the other side of the town, in an old-fashioned hotel, with panelled doors, and swords hung at angles on the walls. David Rhys Jones told me that the last time he was in Ayr he stayed in a hotel where the service and the attitude were so bad that he and Donald Newby booked out after two days. Travel broadens the mind and shortens the patience.

Tuesday 5

We were just finishing our bar suppers tonight when the place began to fill up with bowlers and hangers-on, most of them talking too loudly, and some, inevitably, too fat, carrying what a late bowler friend of mind was fond of calling brewer's goitre. This was our signal to leave, as we don't agree that you have to shout in order to enjoy yourself.

Weather fine today. Colin Best, of whom few have heard outside Ireland, won the singles. From his general appearance I thought he might be a civil servant. It turns out he's a taxi driver in Belfast.

Thursday 7

Same hotel, same bar suppers. A girl singer came forward at eight o'clock and we braced ourselves for the worst. However, she had quite a mellifluous voice for one of her type and we sat out three numbers before departing. Most of the diners were in the over-fifty age group but seemed to enjoy the music, though it was hardly the kind of thing they would have been brought up on.

Irrelevant or not, I told Ruth the true story that Pat Sullivan once told me, of the jazz-loving friend of his who went to a classical concert and was escorted from the hall after he had leapt to his feet at the exciting conclusion of a symphony, shouting, "Sock it to 'em, Beethoven baby!" That man's reaction must be one of the sincerest tributes ever paid to Ludwig van – and look what happened.

Traversed Oswald Road and the railway bridge to get the full effect of the sunset beyond the islands in the Clyde. It must be frustrating for the residents to have such a prospect perpetually hidden from them by rolling-stock.

Sunday 10

My annual visit to Aberdeen, my home city. Still Aberdeen, despite the oil. Looked at it through eyes that had recently read an essay by Lewis Grassic Gibbon associating granite with alleged defects in the Aberdonian character, and decided that you could do the same with igloos and Eskimos or mud huts and jungle dwellers, and be just as "right" or "wrong." Not very original, that, I know, but there you are.

Drove up Deeside to Durris, refreshing ourselves at a tea shack named Cairn Mon Earn ("Hill with Rocks"), run by a lady who was once a belly-dancer. Mist and rain clouds somehow enhanced the view towards Banchory. A TV mast nearby – incongruous.

Monday 11

To Ballater, a place first seen by me at the beginning of the war, when my sister and I were evacuated to the country. Lunch at a church, long disused, that's been converted into a hotel, and a good one too. Still feeding the five thousand, you might say. Have never seen so many objects and trinkets and mementoes in one place – some from Africa; perhaps the idea is that the multiplicity of objects, occupying every other foot of space, will disguise the fact that the building used to be a church. If so, why? Guilt?

In the afternoon we strolled up the Braemar road, returning by the lower path, beside the Dee. This path would have carried the railway from Ballater to Braemar had Queen Victoria not forbidden it. Ballater she decreed to be far enough. Beyond it, at Balmoral, her privacy was sacrosanct. Things have changed.

Friday 15

There was an eleven-year-old boy, Matthew Woodcock, in the pairs final of the Eastbourne open tournament. He and his father, Arthur, are from the St Fagans club in Cardiff, and they lost to Chris Turrell and Ollie Ovett, a nephew of the athlete, from Brighton. The lad has ample confidence and most of the gestures. Could be one to watch out for.

As often happens at these tournaments, a player coming through to the final stages in more than one event threatened confusion in the timetabling. Keith Bailey, from Hayes in Middlesex, got into the singles and pairs semi-finals and decided to scratch from the singles so as not to let his partner down. His reward was to lose both the pairs and the plate match for the losing singles semi-finalists. Peter Pullen of Bellingham won the singles.

A funfair alongside the Princes Park greens made an unwelcome sight and sound for competitors and spectators during the week. "What a place and what a time to have it," the tournament organisers said, and protested to the corporation, who promised not to let such a conflict of interests occur again.

Saturday 16

Fish and chips again in the Lemon Tree Cafe at Ferring. Have never seen so many cars in the car park, yet the cafe was half empty. At the far end of Ilex Way, near Fernhurst Drive, we found a recreation ground, secluded, where a cricket match was proceeding. Turned out to be the third teams of Goring and Littlehampton.

A lady spectator told us she had recently been talking with the parks ranger when he learned over his mobile telephone that a stag was loose in Durrington cemetery. It had been hit by a car, breaking a leg, and was crazed with pain. Four strong men were needed. The animal was sedated with a dart and probably destroyed.

Sunday 17

While two billion people watched the World Cup final, we walked the dogs in Beddington Park.

Wednesday 20

I see that *The Oldie* magazine is to close. In its short life it tried a sports column, which was soon dropped. There was a feeble piece on bowls, all about the age range in the game, and how it is getting more and more popular with the younger set. What, again? Surely some fresher viewpoint than that could have been dreamt up. Still, *The Oldie* is – was – a very readable magazine. Perhaps it was too different to survive. Blandness is all now.

This evening my first, probably last, club friendly of the season, against Worcester Park. Returned home to a cold bath – much needed in the present weather.

Saturday 23

Tournament season in full swing. Eastbourne past; Bournemouth, Worthing and Broadstairs to come (there would be

Hastings too, if it didn't coincide with the EBA championships). My ideal summer would be spent touring England and playing, say, six tournaments, in the company of three likeminded friends, so that we could all enter, individually or as teams. For me it would also mean writing, supplying results to the paper, and marking. Some day, perhaps, some day.

Middlesex beat Hampshire at Chesham in the last eight of the Middleton Cup, six shots the difference. One Hampshire rink dropped a seven around the sixteenth end, and afterwards it was said, and repeated, that this cost their county the match. Logical, maybe, but unfair, as there were nearly thirty ends left to play across the green at the time, and, anyway, that same unfortunate rink scored a redeeming five later.

Tuesday 26

Visited Donald Newby, who lives in Halesworth. He had a stroke two years ago, almost losing the use of his right hand, and he can do little journalistic work now. Introduced to his brother Derek, the president of the Suffolk Bowling Association this year, who said the Halesworth Angel green is the best in the county. Would've liked a chance to test it.

I reminded Donald of our first meeting – in the Bowl Inn at Beach House Park in 1981, while sheltering from a rainstorm during the internationals. He was editing *World Bowls* then and invited me to write for it. Can't exactly remember my first contribution, but fancy it was a frivolous piece about bowls terminology.

Friday 29

Among the mail awaiting me at home, copies of *The Green*, Canada's national bowls magazine. Shawn Bittner gives my book a nice mention in her editorial.

Mafeking has been relieved. *The Oldie* has been resuscitated – as a monthly instead of a fortnightly.

August

Tuesday 2

The winners of the Bournemouth open singles constitute a roll-call of some of the finest players, from Fred Horn in 1962 (to go no further back), through Peter Line, Jock McAtee, Harold Powell, Harry Reston, Alan Windsor, Jim Morgan, Charlie Burch, Robert Provan, John Ottaway and Tony Allcock, to David Ward (for the second time) in 1992. The champion one year all too often makes a rapid exit the next, and it came to pass this time with the defeat of Chris Daniels by Ron Thomas in the first round.

Familiar faces greet me in the committee room – Jack Fincher, Vic Larkman, Dick Hallett, Bob Grimsdale. I've been in their debt annually since my first visit to Meyrick Park in 1982. Vic's *sotto voce* humour is as quick as ever. Dick Jones used to run the tournament with relaxed authority; Tony Dayman, the secretary now, does an equally good job in a quieter style. "Brought your chalk?" they ask. "A whole stick," I reply; and I'm on rink ten as marker tomorrow morning, at nine sharp, after breakfast in the Meyrick cafeteria.

Thursday 4

Marked two games. The first was won by Dorian Bishop, a graduate of the Peter Line school of bowling, having led frequently for Line in the Worthing tournament – and elsewhere, for all I know. The second winner was Jack

Nicky Jones (right) congratulates his partner, Chris Stanger, on a good bowl during the final of the Bournemouth tournament pairs at Meyrick Park. They were the eventual winners. (Photograph: John Beasley)

Waterfield, from the Bournville club in Birmingham, who deserved an extra large bar of chocolate for turning 8–15 into 21–20. That second game was a particular pleasure to mark.

Continuing talk about the possibility of building another indoor club in the Bournemouth area. They were talking about one on Spion Kop, across the road from the Meyrick greens, twelve years ago, I recall. But it is still only talk. The council, according to Julian Haines, erstwhile England bowler and now the proprietor of a bowls shop in Winton, is too slow to catch a cold. I suppose that if the sport had been football or baseball or golf or greyhound racing, a decision in favour would have been made long ago. As ever, bowls remains at the tail of the queue.

Saturday 6

Griff Sanders, the singles winner, is scarcely the purist's idea of a bowler. He's twenty-one, his hair is in a pony-tail, he wears his cap back to front, and he gleefully rolls up his white trousers to reveal grey socks. He often turns his back on a bowl after delivery, walking away to talk to spectators; but whereas with most players that indicates a bad bowl, with Sanders it means it will end up as the shot. To this cocksureness he added casual-seeming accuracy, and the combination was too much for all his opponents, none more so than Wayne Garnett, 21–5 loser in the final.

Sanders lives in Torquay and belongs to the Newton Abbot club. Asked about previous achievements on the green, he replied: "I once won a penny-on-the-jack competition at my club." Having had his little joke, however, he said he's a junior international indoors and has skipped a Teignbridge four to the EIBA quarter-finals at Melton Mowbray.

He was gratified, in an innocent sort of way, when Jimmy Davidson told him that David Bryant and Percy Baker had never won the Bournemouth singles, reckoned by some to be harder than the EBA. And now he, Sanders, had done it at his first go.

Playing on their home green, Chris Stanger and Nicky Jones won the pairs against Jack Davies and Brian Miller.

Monday 8

One of my most depressing experiences was to board the London train at Worthing in the middle of August, see shaven heads as far as the eye could reach, and realize with horrible suddenness that the football season had just begun. That was a while ago, but I remember it too well.

On Saturday, at the conclusion of the Bournemouth finals, Colin Marshall of Radio Solent rang his editor to ask if they'd like an interview with the singles winner. "No, thanks," he was told. "The football season starts next week and we're full up with interviews." Having listened to Griff Sanders, and either listened to or read the comments of footballers and their managers, I'm sure that Sanders, being fresh and uncynical instead of professional and jaded, would have been ten times better value.

Tuesday 9

To Muswell Hill to have a tooth filled. I've been with the same dentist for over thirty years, having continued as a patient of his after leaving the district to live in Carshalton, on the opposite side of London. I lived in Muswell Hill for seventeen years, and going back there at any time, for whatever reason, is a sentimental journey.

It was, among many other things, where I learned the game of bowls. My first club, North Middlesex, at the foot of Muswell Hill itself, with Alexandra Palace on the skyline, is defunct now, the pavilion gone. There's an overgrown path along one side, leading from Wood Vale to Park Road, and stopping to peer through the broken fencing I saw that what had been the green is now covered in weeds.

Wednesday 10

While most of the bowls press were making their way to Canada for the Commonwealth Games, I was making my way to Worthing for the open tournament – in which, if the truth were known, there's probably much greater interest among the bowling public. Stopped at Steyning for refreshments and called on Charles Macdonald, who has a music bookshop in the town. He's just been appointed organist to Sussex University. He's still sweeping the streets of Steyning first thing in the morning to make a bit of extra money; the shop's not doing well. "It's the only physical exercise I get," he says.

I bought from him Michael Kennedy's *Portrait of Elgar*. Then on to Worthing, where the hotel have put us in the honeymoon suite. A four-poster with a sea view.

Thursday 11

Arundel this morning. More tourists than natives. Marked a singles in the afternoon. One of the players, Eddie Shew, belongs to the Carshalton Beeches club, where I've played. He was 16-5 down, led 20-18, and lost to Justin Davis, from Holt in Wiltshire.

Saturday 13

I thought Lee Dickson would win the singles. He's a past Surrey champion and I once saw him give Tony Allcock a hard game in the nationals. But he lost to Malcolm Dare, who went on to beat Barry Dixon fairly easily in the final. Dare's from Leicester originally and moved to Torquay twenty years ago. Understand he's a good tennis player, too. He told me he ran John Wickham close in the Devon singles this season – and Wickham won the EBA title last year. So much, anyway, for my Dickson hunch. I really must stop tipping *anybody* to win in this game. I ought to have learnt that lesson many moons ago.

Sunday 14

Played in the fours drive, successfully instituted at the tournament last season. Five games of seven ends each. Wasn't among the original competitors, but there were enough reserves to make up additional teams, and I found myself with a (lady) second from Egham, a third from Horley, and a skip from Crawley. Lost our first four games and

Jock Munro (left) and the author at Beach House Park, 1981.

won the fifth. Pleasant way to pass the Sabbath. Weather perfect.

Wednesday 17

Some of the bowlers who stayed at the Delmar Hotel last year are here again, including four from Enfield and two from Hemel Hempstead. One of the Hemel Hempsteadites mentioned that he was born and raised in Finchley and lived opposite Margaret Thatcher before she was famous, or notorious.

Am out of the pairs and fours already. I joined up with Stan Snowdon, from Didcot, whose partner had had to withdraw, and we lost an enjoyable match by three shots to a pair from Cheam Village, a club with what's reputed to be one of the best greens in Surrey; I can vouch for that, having played there a few times. Our four was made up more or less at the last minute – Stan and I, and two Lancing bowlers, Jim Hughes and Tony Barrett. We did well for a while against a Mid-Surrey lot skipped by Paul Reeves, but couldn't sustain our effort.

Thursday 18

Met Jock Munro for the first time in twelve months. He has had two strokes this year, has lost the use of his right arm, and walks with a stick. And I met him at the same spot in Beach House Park where I first met him in 1981, when he was head greenkeeper and famous in his line, restlessly energetic and sociable. What a change. Jock served in the Seaforth Highlanders in the war, winning a Military Medal in North Africa – receiving it, I believe, from the hands of Montgomery himself. A widow in Bath Road looks after him now. Jock thought bowls a simple game, and he was a county standard player. He took a satirical attitude towards theories like controlled weight, and we often joked about it.

Stan Snowdon and I lost to George Hewetson and Malcolm Dare, the singles winner, in the consolation pairs. Dare's mother is with him at the tournament, watching from a deckchair; she's an alert, smiling lady, in her ninetieth year, who can remember riding in one of the earliest motor cars to appear on the streets of Leicester, around 1913. After the match she said to me: "My husband used to say, 'Always play for love of the game.' "

John Ward, who helps John Holliman run the tournament, remarked today: "I absolutely hate gardening. Can't see the point in it." "Join the club, John," I said. I don't quite hate gardening, though: I just dislike and resent it. If I were single, I'd live in a flat, without so much as a window-box.

Saturday 20

Driving home, we caught a glimpse of the eccentric Horace on the outskirts of Worthing – at least I think Horace is his name. He materializes most years at Beach House Park during the national championships, riding a bicycle on the central walkway, wearing a Maurice Chevalier (or Archie Rice) straw hat, a Union Jack round his waist, spats, and twirling a silver-topped cane. When not mounted, he walks in an affected manner, perhaps imagining himself as the man who broke the bank at Monte Carlo. I'm told he can be very abusive if you say the wrong thing in his hearing.

One of the security officers in the park said that Horace is fond of standing in the middle of the road at Durrington directing the traffic. Come to think of it, he was near traffic lights when he saw him. Probably waiting to go on point duty. I wonder what experience in life, if any, turned him into what he has become.

Programme for the EBA championships among the mail awaiting me when I arrived home. A four from Croydon, skipped by Dave Clark, have qualified; also John Roll from Sutton in the singles, and Paul Vam in the triples. Roll lost to Wynne Richards in the county final – Wynne's fifth win, a Surrey record.

Monday 22

Norman, a neighbour, said he'd been at a car boot fair where a man tried to sell him a set of secondhand bowls for £40, which seemed a reasonable bargain until it was noticed that all four were badly chipped. This reminds me that Stan Snowdon owns eighteen sets of woods, by far the biggest number I've heard of in the possession of one bowler. He doesn't use them all; he just likes collecting things. I know of a bowler who carries two sets of woods, two mats and two jacks in his car boot wherever he goes, so that, if he happens to pass a bowling club and feels like a few ends, he has everything he requires.

Wednesday 24

The Commonwealth Games bowls is not prominent in the papers. Results yes, text negligible. Even the results inadequate, with no players' names given in the singles, only countries. The old story.

Thursday 25

I have noted, so far, two reactions to mention of my book (*Bowling Enchanted Woods*). The first is bright interest in the fact that it has been published. The second is thinly concealed disappointment at the subject. Bowls? Most faces have fallen when I uttered the word. The unspoken thought must be: why didn't he do a bestseller full of sex and violence? Or perhaps: why didn't he do one about a "real" sport – meaning, say, soccer?

It's impossible not to feel a little downhearted about all this, until I remind myself that writing the book and achieving publication (at painfully long last) are what matter, and blow the subject. If they want sex and violence, let them read Wilbur Smith, or whoever. If they want soccer, let them read the *Sun*. But if they want bowls, let them read me, if only to discover that the game *can* be dragged away from technicalities and related to the wider world.

Having got that off my chest, I promise not to mention the book again.

Sunday 28

I've just read in the local paper of a bowler who killed himself by jumping off the Ramsgate–Ostend ferry carrying a case containing (it is understood) his woods.

Monday 29

Returning to Worthing for the EBA championships, I hear that
Jock Munro has died.

Tuesday 30

Val Doonican, Richard Digance, George Melly, Danny La
Rue, John Mann at the Pavilion Theatre – not together,
you understand. Some things change little from August to
August. Crowded dining-rooms in the big hotels – the Beach,
the Chatsworth, the Ardington – with their windows open to
the soft evening air, bring back my apprentice years on the
bowls circuit, when, walking past, I would imagine a score of
ends being excitedly re-enacted over the coffee and liqueurs,
each skip seeking to outmatch his neighbour in describing
his own inimitable brilliance in drawing the shot when the
other team held eight on the twentieth. I still catch myself
imagining it all, with a smile. And walking past the pubs –
those bowlers' resorts, the Egremont and the Royal Oak – I
have only to substitute beer and sandwiches for coffee and
liqueurs, though it may well be that in the pubs the descriptive
details are more highly coloured.

September

Thursday 1

Tony Allcock won the fours with Cheltenham – a first for him
and a first for any Gloucestershire club in that event. Saying
a few words afterwards, he recommended cod liver oil, the
product of the sponsors, Sanatogen, for jet lag. He played his
first round on Tuesday, a few hours after arriving home from
Canada, and on his biographical form, in the section for other
items of interest, wrote: "Horses. Jet lag!"

The proprietor of the Chipwick said Allcock and companions had been there the previous evening. I made some remark about a big catch for a fish restaurant.

David Rhys Jones turned up today, fresh – or not so fresh – from Canada. He said his journalistic routine over there, which included filing reports at five in the morning, sometimes left him feeling, as he put it, "knackered with an f." Worthing will seem like a rest cure.

Press room not the same since the loss of Jane Adams. She ran it for the previous sponsors, the Woolwich Building Society, and ran it very efficiently. In the beginning she knew nothing about bowls or press liaison, but she learned, and grew into the job. Patrick Sullivan did it last season. So far there's no replacement, or if there is we haven't noticed.

Friday 2

A spectator died at Beach House Park today while her son-in-law was playing in the triples. When he was told, he passed out, falling on a bowl and injuring his back.

Sunday 4

Sixty! My very own swinging sixties – I hope. Do I feel sixty? To which there are two replies – "No" and "How does sixty *feel*, exactly?" I don't feel any age, just alive and well, apart from stiffness in the back first thing in the morning. Bought a booklet entitled *Your Birthday* from Smith's, which informs me that Virgoans "usually prefer to keep a low profile." That's me. It's a privilege of sorts, also, to have the same birthday as Anton Bruckner and Tom Watson.

We walked to Goring and back in the morning – a round journey of about four miles, I'd guess. Saw an old Catalina flying-boat low over the sea; it was from the Shoreham air show, and they say it's the only one still in existence.

Torquay won the triples – the first Devon club to do it, as per Cheltenham for Gloucestershire in the fours. The final was a subdued affair in one sense, all the decibels coming from Cumbria and Northamptonshire in the under-25 double fours: decibels, plus high-fives and histrionics – "Pick it up!" "Jack!" "Clean!" "Solid!" They should set it to dance music.

Tuesday 6

David Johnson won the Leamington Spa tournament twice in the 1960s. "I got the same prize money – fifteen guineas – as Christine Truman did for losing the Wimbledon final," he told us. In modern values that would scarcely cover bed and breakfast for one night at the EBA championships.

Nearly forgot to say that David Hunn was down at Worthing last Saturday to write one of his graceful "minority sport" pieces for the *Sunday Times*. David was once sports editor of the *Observer*, where he had to cope with Hugh McIlvanney. "What a lift it would give to bowls," he remarked, "if McIlvanney came here and did two thousand words about it." We agreed, although I'm not, myself, an admirer of McIlvanney's style, which I find ponderous. But there's no gainsaying his reputation.

Wednesday 7

Hail and rain in the morning, with thunder over in the Littlehampton direction, cleared into a lovely fresh afternoon. Players from Ponteland (pronounced Pon*tee*land) in Newcastle won the pairs with the utmost ease. Must be the first final of which I didn't watch a single complete end; the singles prelims on adjacent greens were too diverting.

Twenty-four hours ago I was what my mother used to call "thick in the clear" with a streaming cold. Somewhat better now. Have started taking cod liver oil tablets, not to ingratiate myself with the sponsors, but because I think they'll do me good.

Friday 9

Brett Morley's one of those dour, rounded, persistent players that I've always felt certain would win the national singles some day. Today he did – the first winner from a Nottinghamshire club. He beat Paul Wilkinson, the first finalist from a Derbyshire club, though he lives over the border in Nottingham, four miles from Morley himself. Somebody said Morley was almost in tears afterwards. Towards the end of the match, while Wilkinson was keeping Morley in suspense for the winning shot, I chanced to find myself standing beside Wilkinson's father, who said: "My boy never gives up." I could see that. Both Derbyshire qualifiers got into the last eight – a rare, perhaps unique, occurrence, since Derbyshire is hardly a power in the game.

What happened to Tony Allcock? He lost in the second round to Graham Hatherall, a Swindon southpaw, who then went out in his next match. Allcock was inclined to blame the rink (B4, in case you're curious) for his defeat. It never ceases to amaze me how often the rink is made the ogre, and how rarely you hear a player say defeat was due at least partly to his own inadequacies. You'd think that, win or lose, someone of Allcock's consummate skill would find ways of unlocking the secrets of *any* rink.

Saturday 10

Harry Haynes is staying at the Delmar Hotel. He was runner-up to Charlie Graham in the 1963 EBA singles, and he told me that Charlie died a fortnight ago. Harry, who's eighty-two now, played for England indoors and out – indoors as second to David Bryant, with Jim Girdwood and Len Kirton completing the rink.

Emotion in the air as Cumbria win the Middleton Cup for the first time, by four shots over Middlesex. A slight transformation from last year, when Cumbria lost by seventy-two to Kent.

Sunday 11

To Brighton for the morning, the Kemp Town end, Hove and the centre being nearer Worthing and so a little more familiar to us. Idly, I fancied a top-floor flat in one of the terraces looking across to France. Noted Anna Neagle and Lewis Carroll among those who have had similar ideas. "It's Bath by the sea," Joy said.

Met Malcolm Dare and his mother in the Bowl Inn. "She's just been round the putting green in seventy-eight strokes," he said. "Now she wants to go back and beat her record." Champion stuff from someone in her ninetieth year.

Monday 12

Back to basics. The Broadstairs tournament. No "superstars," just bowlers. Results by phone from Harry Gold or Lew Bing. I'm going there Thursday to Saturday this week and Friday-Saturday next week. Looking down the names of past winners, you see Doreen Hankin in 1990; she won the national indoor singles two years later.

Thursday 15

Foul weather for the journey to Broadstairs. Journey not so jolly, either. Train fifteen minutes late leaving Victoria – driver missing, presumed alive – and then broke down at Westgate – something to do with a defect in the second coach, the one I happened to be in. Sat for twenty-five minutes, while various BR people hurried to and fro in the pelting rain, before moving stealthily towards Margate, with the smoothest start of the run.

Gloom of a sort at the guest-house, too. They've had a mediocre season business-wise and the area is "dead as a pancake" – the phrase of Dennis Hurst, the owner. "Would you believe it," he said, "they hope to revive things by rebuilding Margate pier, which was badly damaged in the 1987 gales. A pier! Crikey, they need more than that round here."

Friday 16

A better day, dry, but with a keen wind that made bowls, watching or playing, a mixed pleasure. At breakfast two men seated at another table were discussing their trip to Dunkirk yesterday. A very ordinary place, was their opinion. They had gone into the cathedral, mainly to shelter from the rain, which prevented them sitting in pavement cafes to help pass the time.

This evening dined again at the Riviera, a pleasant Italian restaurant on the High Street. Music from *The Big Country* in the background again. Last night a couple on the opposite side of the room brightened up as soon as they recognized it, telling each other what it was. Tonight a different couple in the same seats did exactly the same. And under my breath I added the cast – Gregory Peck, Charlton Heston, Jean Simmons, Burl Ives – and the director, William Wyler. Cheap music is potent, as Noel Coward said (didn't he?), and nothing wrong with that, I say.

Saturday 17

Bleak weather in the town of Bleak House for the singles finals. A wind cold enough for November, the few spectators huddled in coats, scarves and rugs. Clay Tingey from Margate won for the second year, although Don Briscoe, a local man, had his chance at 20–18 before delivering three woods a yard or more short, virtually handing the game to Tingey. Mary Webster, having excelled herself in beating Jan Stern, the favourite, in the semi-finals, retained enough of that form to win against Kathleen Leeder. Mrs Stern was a losing finalist in the national pairs at Leamington, and she and her husband, Ted, lost the mixed pairs final here to Tingey and Maisie Trench.

Thursday 22

I've bowled less this summer than in any previous year, and that's going back to 1972, when I started. One reason is that I've been away from home more than usual. Another may be the decline in afternoon play at my club. When I joined in 1981, you could count on two or three roll-ups most afternoons. Now, you're lucky to find enough bodies to make up a pairs.

This is not a general thing; it varies from club to club. Some, particularly if a good proportion of the members are retired, have a healthy turnout in the afternoon. At others the green could just as easily be empty. There is also the attraction of the bar, which some bowlers prefer to the game, and the dislike, amounting almost to disdain, of competitively-minded bowlers for casual bowls. The middle way for me: I enjoy competition – and roll-ups. But then, I'm just an ordinary bowler, and getting more ordinary every day.

Saturday 24

Clay Tingey just failed to become the first man to win the three titles available to him at Broadstairs. He won the singles and mixed pairs, as aforementioned, but lost the men's pairs. Before that third final, he'd been playing so well that somebody said that if he'd worn a skirt he'd have won the women's singles and pairs also.

As usual at these tournaments, one or two of the losing semi-finalists went home early, for this reason or that, leaving the organizers in an embarrassing position at the prizegiving ceremony, with the mayor (a lady) present. Harry Gold, the secretary, visibly put out by it all. Next year is the golden jubilee of the tournament.

Sunday 25

To Old Colfeians for the national mixed pairs. Sat beside Maurice Phillips's widow at lunch. Maurice played for England and is said to be the man who taught Gary Smith the game. Old Colfeians used to be Gary's club, of course, until he went to wider fame at Blackheath and Greenwich.

Not much animation on the green during the final, and even less off it. They say that when people have nothing else to do, they eat to pass the time, though they may not be hungry. Observation of bowls spectators bears this out. Biscuits and cakes, quality of, high on the list of subjects I overheard being discussed among the chairs, and it sent me indoors to buy tea and cake for myself.

Not much animation on the green? Partly it may have been because these bowlers aren't accustomed to playing in front of a crowd, even one as small as today's, and feel inhibited. They showed plenty of skill but kept emotional display to a minimum – and that's an overstatement.

Thursday 28

Watched the bowls from Preston on TV. So did my mother-in-law, who's in her ninetieth year and almost chairbound. She opened her eyes for fully a minute before relapsing into her customary doze. Presumably one bowl was enough for her.

Friday 30

Deborah Kerr, Johnny Mathis and Sir Peter Yarranton, chairman of the Sports Council, have their birthdays today, which is also the anniversary of the birth of Truman Capote and Marc Bolan and of the death of Rudolf Diesel and James Dean. Also it's the end of the outdoor bowling season. Next week I start on the new carpet at Croydon. I don't expect it'll make much difference to my game. I'm consistent in my inconsistency.

Bowling green

Hedged round with privet
As with habit and with age,
Move the bowlers
On the lawn that is their stage.

Their gestures inflame the air
Like impatient clouds
Gathering to some point far away
That the sunset shrouds

And weighs with red.
The arm swings forward while the eye
Is calm that contemplates the speed.
Marvellous, the silent rounded cry

Of motion, ending
In collision.
Then come measuring-tapes,
Disagreement and confusion.

Is this Olympus where the gods
Spin the dark planets, holding fate
In hands tobacco-stained?
Or can they only hope the bowl runs straight?

Lucy Barker, age 17
James Allen's Girls' School
Dulwich, London, 1990

From *The Best of Children's Poetry*, ed. Jennifer Curry (Red Fox, Random House Children's Books).